Enterprise Investment Scheme

And Other Venture Capital Reliefs

Andrew Rainford

Disclaimer

This edition May 2018
First edition (published as *Venture Capital Schemes*) February 2016

Enterprise Investment Scheme

And Other Venture Capital Reliefs

Andrew Rainford

Published by:

Claritax Books Ltd
6 Grosvenor Park Road
Chester, CH1 1QQ

www.claritaxbooks.com

ISBN: 978-1-912386-04-8

Other titles from Claritax Books

Other tax titles from Claritax Books include:

- A-Z of Plant & Machinery
- Advising British Expats
- Capital Allowances
- Construction Industry Scheme
- Discovery Assessments
- Employee Benefits & Expenses
- Employment Status
- Entrepreneurs' Relief
- Financial Planning with Trusts
- Furnished Holiday Lettings
- Main Residence Relief
- Pension Tax Guide
- Research & Development
- Residence: The Definition in Practice
- Stamp Duty Land Tax
- Tax Chamber Hearings
- Tax Losses
- VAT Registration

See www.claritaxbooks.com for details of these and of our other forthcoming titles.

About the author

Andrew Rainford BA (Hons), ATT, CTA is an experienced tax adviser, author and publishing editor based in North Wales. After graduating with first class honours with a degree in accounting and finance from the University of Wales in 2005, Andrew worked in the field of public sector audit until switching to tax in December 2007 – just in time for a busy January.

Andrew trained and qualified with the independent London firm Rees Pollock, before joining Ernst & Young's personal tax centre as a consultant, becoming one of the foremost specialists in EIS-related work. During his time in practice, Andrew regularly contributed to various professional publications, including *Taxation* magazine, the *Practical Tax Newsletter, Tolleys Tax Guidance, Tolleys Tax Digest* and *Tax for Professionals.*

Making the decision to go into writing and publishing full time, Andrew became editor in chief of Indicator's *Tax for Professionals* publication in June 2015, and a contributory editor to *Whiteman and Sherry on Income Tax and Capital Gains Tax.*

Andrew still undertakes consultancy work on an ad hoc basis, through his company Red Dragon. He can be contacted by email at Andrew@reddragontax.co.uk.

About the publisher

Claritax Books publishes specialist tax titles, complementing what is on offer from the larger tax publishers. Typically, our books cover niche topics in greater depth or take a more practical approach to particular tax issues. Our titles are written for accountants (both in-house and in practice), tax advisers, employers, lawyers and other professionals. Our authors include barristers, solicitors, accountants and other experienced tax specialists.

Claritax Books titles cover (among other topics) tax appeals, capital allowances, the statutory residence rules, CGT reliefs, the CIS scheme, pensions and trusts, stamp duty land tax, VAT, employment taxes and furnished holiday lettings. Visit www.claritaxbooks.com for details of all our books.

Claritax Books is a trading name of Claritax Books Ltd (company number 07658388, VAT number 114 9371 20). The company is based in Chester, England.

Abbreviations

AIF	Alternative Investment Fund
AIM	Alternative Investment Market
BES	Business expansion scheme
CG	(HMRC's) Capital Gains Manual
CGT	Capital gains tax
Ch.	Chapter
CVS	Corporate venturing scheme
EC	European Commission
EIS	Enterprise investment scheme
EU	European Union
FA	Finance Act
FCA	Financial Conduct Authority
FSA	Financial Services Authority
HMRC	HM Revenue & Customs
ISDX	ICAP Securities and Derivatives Exchange
ITA 2007	Income Tax Act 2007
ITEPA 2003	Income Tax (Earnings & Pensions) Act 2003
ITTOIA 2005	Income Tax (Trading & Other Income) Act 2005
LLP	Limited liability partnership
Para.	Paragraph
PAYE	Pay As You Earn
Pt.	Part
QCB	Qualifying corporate bond
S.	Section
SCEC	Small Companies Enterprise Centre
Sch.	Schedule
SDLT	Stamp duty land tax
SEIS	Seed enterprise investment scheme
SI	Statutory instrument
SITR	Social investment tax relief
TC	Tax Chamber
TCGA 1992	Taxation of Chargeable Gains Act 1992
TIOPA 2010	Taxation (International and Other Provisions) Act 2010
TMA 1970	Taxes Management Act 1970
UKFTT	United Kingdom First-tier Tribunal
VCM	(HMRC's) Venture Capital Schemes Manual
VCT	Venture capital trust

Foreword

There is a real need for this book among professionals who are called upon to advise taxpayers about tax efficient investments, which are widely advertised, but little understood. The approach taken here is to break each scheme down into manageable chunks and explain it in plain English, so the details can be understood by all. This will help not only tax and financial advisers, but also the individual investors who need to take personal responsibility for investment choices they make.

Taxpayers who have funds to invest want their money to work hard, rather than passively accumulate small amounts of interest in deposit accounts. The steady options for active investing for the medium to long term have traditionally been: property, pension funds, and the stock market.

Investing in property has been in vogue for some years, but changes to income tax relief for mortgage interest on residential property, and increased land transaction duties on property purchases, are making that avenue less attractive. The scope for investing in pension funds has also been curtailed as the annual allowance is a maximum of £40,000, reduced to £10,000 for very high earners.

Individual investors, who have some appetite for risk, are turning to peer-to-peer lending and to equity investments in smaller companies. The latter category of venture capital investment, if structured correctly, can allow the investor to benefit from one or more tax reliefs.

The venture capital schemes detailed in this book enable well-advised investors to reduce their income tax or capital gains liabilities. But in every case the tax relief is dependent on getting all the details of the investment right, so that it falls neatly within the scheme rules. One small deviation for the investment plan, perhaps by repaying a loan or issuing the wrong type of shares, can scupper the tax relief for all the investors.

This book carefully takes apart the qualifying conditions for each venture capital scheme, and identifies the conditions which are essential for each type of tax relief. This is important, as some investors are only interested in income tax relief, others in the capital gains reliefs, while a third group may want to take maximum advantage of both.

The qualifying conditions must also be met for defined periods, normally extending to three years after the date of the investment. If the adviser fails to support and monitor the company's activities throughout that key period, HMRC may withdraw approval for the venture capital scheme and the tax relief is lost. Any deviation from the company's investment plan can be a very expensive mistake for its investors, and may result in professional indemnity claims for the advisers.

Studying this book won't guarantee that the chosen venture capital investment plans will succeed, but it may ensure that those plans don't fail for the wrong reasons.

Rebecca Cave FCA MBA CTA

Director: Taxwriter Ltd

Preface

I am delighted to introduce the second edition of my first full-length reference title, which I hope will prove to be both accessible and informative.

The tax reliefs offered by venture capital type schemes, or risk finance investments as they are also sometimes called, are a very powerful tool in any adviser's planning arsenal.

With wholesale changes to dividend taxation since 2016, and further erosion of their tax efficiency with the cut in the dividend allowance from April 2018, EIS and VCT investments could well become more popular, as small business owners investigate alternative ways to protect their hard-earned profits.

Because the reliefs are generous, they are subject to a plethora of qualifying conditions and anti-avoidance provisions, which at first can seem utterly confusing to the general practitioner. Relief can be denied for what appear to be desirable commercial arrangements, and so it is essential to have a good knowledge of the legislation and of how it is applied in practice.

In this volume, I attempt to provide as comprehensive an explanation of the relevant law as possible, based on my experience in practice, as well as my professional interpretation of the provisions.

Tax advisers, accountants and solicitors should of course refrain from advising on specific investments – i.e. making recommendations as to which shares to invest in. To do this requires FCA authorisation, and so ensuring you have at least one financial adviser among your professional contacts, familiar with the schemes to which you can potentially refer clients, is key.

Both the SEIS and SITR derive from the pre-existing EIS legislation. As a result, the provisions for SEIS and SITR are in places identical (or at least similar enough to make little practical difference) to the equivalent under EIS.

I was therefore presented with the choice between adopting a similar approach in this text – which could give the appearance of a certain level of repetition – or of making a high level of cross references to the EIS chapters. I have decided that the former option is more suited to the text, as I was keen for each of the four sections to be able to stand alone. I also personally find it extremely irritating when, in trying to check a technical point, I am constantly needing to flick to various other pages in the text to find an answer, when a simple short paragraph would have been sufficient.

This second edition reflects the changes made by the Finance Acts in 2016, 2017 and 2018.

I would like to thank Ray Chidell for continuing to support and publish this book.

This publication is dedicated to the memory of my friend and colleague Jonathan (JT) Thomas (surely the most devoted Celtic FC fan ever to come out of Merthyr Tydfil), who would have undoubtedly offered to proof-read it and make amendments with his distinctive green pen.

The law is stated as at 6 April 2018.

Andrew Rainford

April 2018

Table of contents

Enterprise Investment Scheme

* What is EIS/SEIS?

*

1. Introduction and background

1.1 History

The Enterprise Investment Scheme (EIS) as we know it today was first introduced in 1994, succeeding the Business Expansion Scheme (BES), which was devised in 1983. The EIS offers generous tax breaks to those who purchase shares which qualify for it.

Both the EIS and the BES before it were seen as a potential solution to the difficulty that entrepreneurs had in obtaining finance from traditional institutions, by offering tax incentives for outsiders investing in private companies, thereby providing much needed working capital. As Sir Geoffrey Howe said during his 1983 Budget:

> "These proposals will transform the position of unquoted trading companies seeking outside equity. It is a further move towards removing the bias in the tax system against the personal shareholder and a further measure to encourage wider share ownership. By concentrating help on those companies which do not have ready access to outside capital, the scheme will assist many more small or medium companies to realise their undoubted potential for growth."

The BES was, however, widely drawn – the range of potential investors and investee companies led to investments qualifying for the scheme being made mainly for tax sheltering, rather than genuine commercial reasons. The EIS was introduced in 1994 to bring things back into line with the original stated objectives. Speaking at the time, Michael Portillo said:

> "The purpose of Enterprise Investment Schemes [sic] is to recognise that unquoted trading companies can often face considerable difficulties in realising relatively small amounts of share capital. The new scheme is intended to provide a well-targeted means for some of those problems to be overcome."

1.2 Widening the scope

As mentioned above, the EIS tightened up many of the qualifying conditions that existed under the BES. This was in turn criticised as excluding too many companies from qualifying, and so in 2012 several changes were announced relaxing some of these measures so as to be more inclusive. One announced measure was to increase the maximum amount a company could receive under EIS in any 12 month period from £2 million to £10 million. Unfortunately this change was rejected as excessive by the European Commission on State Aid. The annual limit was eventually increased to £5 million, where it remains at the time of writing, although FA 2018 increased the limit to £10 million for knowledge-intensive companies.

1.3 Reining in

At the March 2015 Budget, George Osborne – Chancellor of the then Coalition Government – announced that various changes, including a lifetime maximum limit on how much can be raised via the venture capital schemes to supplement the existing annual maximum, were required to the EIS (and other venture capital schemes) to ensure it continued to receive EU State aid approval. At the time of the announcement, the proposed new measures were restrictive, but more generous than the EU Guidelines suggested (subject to EU State aid approval).

Following the Conservative majority at the May 2015 General Election, an emergency budget was announced. On 8 July 2015, the Summer Budget confirmed that the previously announced changes would go ahead; however, they would now more or less follow the EU Guidelines directly, effective from the date of Royal Assent of *Finance (No. 2) Act* 2015 (18 November 2015).

Further changes were announced during the 2017 Autumn Budget that saw relief further restricted. A new qualifying condition now needs to be met for investments following the date of Royal Assent of *Finance Act* 2018, 15 March 2018 (the date specified in the original tax policy note) that will prevent relief where there is little or no real risk to the investor's capital.

Law: F(No.2)A 2015; FA 2018

1.4 EU approval

State aid is prohibited by the *Treaty on the Functioning of the EU* because it can distort competition and affect trade with other member states.

Using taxpayer-funded resources to assist one or more organisations in a way that gives an advantage over others may be State aid, and so is, generally, illegal. There are treaty exemptions for aid schemes which help to achieve the objectives of the community.

The EIS and VCT schemes constitute State aid because of the tax-advantaged investment in the target companies.

The schemes are permitted under treaty exemption, as long as the European Commission approves any changes or modifications to the member state's rules as coming within the parameters of the Community guidelines on State aid to promote risk capital investments in small and medium-sized enterprises.

The guidelines dictate the type of investment that may be approved under the schemes, the size of companies that may benefit and the maximum amount that companies may raise annually.

There are further regulations governing State aid given to a single recipient when its value does not exceed €200,000 (known as *de minimis* aid). The SEIS (see **Chapter 12**) is an example of a scheme governed by these regulations.

1.5 Tax relief under the EIS

1.5.1 Overview

The EIS has four associated tax breaks:

- Income tax relief
- Capital gains tax (CGT) deferral
- CGT exemption
- Loss relief

Each is considered in detail in later chapters but a brief summary is provided below.

1.5.2 Income tax relief

For qualifying investments, relief is given as a tax reduction against the overall liability for the tax year of the investment (or the preceding year). This is therefore applied after other reliefs, such as the personal allowance (if applicable) and personal pension contributions.

The current rate of relief is 30% on up to £1 million (generally) per tax year. Whilst the relief can lead to a refund – for example where tax has already been paid via PAYE – it cannot create a repayment (or further repayment) by reducing the overall tax liability below £nil. The 2017 Budget announced that this annual limit will increase to £2 million for investments into knowledge-intensive companies, and this was confirmed by the *Finance Act* 2018.

Where the relief available exceeds the tax liability for the year of the investment, the possibility of carrying back some or all of the claim into the preceding tax year should be explored.

Example – Alan

Alan makes a qualifying investment of £100,000 in 2018-19. His overall tax liability for the year is £20,000, of which £18,000 has been deducted via PAYE. Alan qualifies for £30,000 of EIS income tax relief, but this will be restricted to £20,000 because he does not have a sufficient tax liability to offset. He will receive a refund of £18,000 and will have no further tax to pay via his self-assessment return, but the additional £10,000 is effectively lost unless it can be carried back to 2017-18.

Law: ITA 2007, s. 158; FA 2018

1.5.3 CGT deferral

Where a qualifying investment is made, the investor can match the amount invested to any capital gains realised in the period beginning three years prior to the EIS investment, and ending one year afterward, and defer the CGT arising on that part of the gain until the EIS shares are disposed of.

Example – Caroline

Caroline (a higher rate taxpayer) makes capital gains after the annual exemption of £250,000 in 2016-17, paying the tax of £70,000 in January 2016. In 2018-19 she makes a qualifying EIS investment of £250,000. If she chooses to, she can match the investment to the £250,000 gains from 2016-17. She would receive a refund of £70,000 and would only have to pay this tax back in the event of a later disposal or disqualifying event.

This relief is particularly valuable as it does not preclude investors who have a connection to the company from claiming it.

Gains which were deferred are brought back into charge at the prevailing rate(s) of tax – currently 10% or 20% depending on other income and gains. Since 3 December 2014, any gains made after that date which would qualify for entrepreneurs' relief at 10% which are deferred under EIS are brought back into charge at 10%. Prior to this the gain would be revived at the prevailing rate.

1.5.4 CGT exemption

Where a claim to EIS income tax relief has been made and not subsequently withdrawn, any gain arising on the EIS shares themselves will not be charged to CGT upon a disposal. It is often not appreciated that any gain deferred will come back into charge in the year of the disposal.

Example – Caroline (continued)

Caroline's investment qualifies for income tax relief which is not withdrawn. The shares are sold on 6 April 2024 for £750,000. The gain of £500,000 is exempt from CGT; however the original £250,000 gain deferred is brought back into charge, and the associated tax, calculated using the applicable rate of CGT (and allowing for any unused annual exemption), is now payable.

1.5.5 Loss relief

Where a qualifying investment is made, and the income tax relief is successfully claimed and not withdrawn, any losses (as adjusted for the income tax relief which is given and not withdrawn) arising on a disposal can be offset against capital gains in the same tax year as the investment (or carried forward against future gains). Alternatively, any such losses can benefit from "share loss relief" under ITA 2007, s. 131 and be offset against general income.

Example – Caroline (further continued)

Suppose, instead, that Caroline's investment only sells for £100,000. She would have a loss of £75,000 (the £150,000 loss less the £75,000 income tax relief not withdrawn) that she could choose to alleviate her other capital gains, or to offset against her general income of the year of disposal or the preceding year.

Ignoring any benefit of the capital gains deferral, it is clear that the risk to the investor (in monetary terms) is significantly reduced by the income tax and loss reliefs. For an additional rate tax payer who makes a failing investment of £100,000, the total relief is £30,000 plus £31,500 ([£100,000 - £30,000] × 45%), meaning that the downside risk of the investment - that is the "true" amount of money actually at stake - is only £38,500 in real cash terms.

In the following chapters we will look at qualifying conditions for the investor and for the investee company, as well as at the general conditions that must be met. We will then look at situations where relief is given but later clawed back.

Law: TCGA 1992, s. 150A; ITA 2007, s. 131

1.6 Claiming relief - process

The issuing company must first complete form EIS1 - the compliance statement - with the relevant details about itself, the nature of its business, and the investments to which EIS relief is intended to apply. HMRC will then consider the application, and provided the tax officer is happy that all qualifying conditions are satisfied HMRC will issue the company with authority to issue EIS certificates to each of the investors. It will enclose blank EIS3 certificates to enable this.

The company will then need to complete the certificates, and issue these to the relevant investors. The investors can then claim tax relief either on their individual tax returns, or by contacting the PAYE office to give effect to relief via their tax codes.

Note that relief cannot be claimed until the certificates are issued. The issuing company can be fined up to £3,000 if it issues certificates without the authority from HMRC, or if it makes a fraudulent or negligent compliance statement.

Advance assurance

It is also possible to request a non-binding opinion, known as advance assurance, from the Small Company Enterprise Centre (SCEC) before the shares are issued by providing them with all details pertinent to the potential investment.

HMRC have long felt that this facility was being strained by speculative enquiries (i.e. ones that are unlikely to lead to an actual investment). This might be done in order to test the boundaries of the legislation, in order to develop tax avoidance schemes for example. In response, in 2017 HMRC undertook a consultation on how to make the service more efficient, and the outcomes were announced in December 2017. In the future it is likely to become possible to submit requests online, which will cut delays owing to postage etc., but in addition, the following streamlining measures have been enacted:

- From 4 December 2017, no opinion will be given if it is apparent that the company is likely to fail to meet the new risk to capital condition (see **4.2.12**).
- From 2 January 2018, no opinion will be given in relation to speculative enquiries. In practice, this means that the company requesting the opinion will need to demonstrate that it has approached potential investors, and will need to provide the names of all individuals, fund managers or other promoters who are expected to invest.
- If a company is relying on a particular interpretation of the law in order to obtain relief, it will need to provide a full technical analysis demonstrating how the requirements of the law are met. HMRC will not issue an opinion unless it believes that the enquiry is seeking to allay genuine concerns (i.e. not simply testing the boundaries of the rules).

An illustration of how the third point might crop up in practice would be contrasting between a company seeking clarification on whether or not a potential investor is connected due to past involvement, and a company sending a number of slightly different scenarios to test the point at which connection is established.

This also applies for Seed EIS advance assurance applications.

Law: ITA 2007, s. 204-208

Guidance: VCM 14000-14210

2. Income tax relief: investor conditions

2.1 Overview

The investor is the person who purchases shares in a company. The decision to do this may be partly influenced by the possibility of EIS relief. Note that the investor does not have to be a serial investor, and the EIS shares could be his or her very first investment.

In practice, if the investment is being made through a financial institution - such as a large financial advisory company - the investor may be required to complete a declaration that he is either a certified high net worth individual, or a self-certified "sophisticated investor". However, neither of these is a formal requirement for qualifying for EIS relief; rather they are requirements to safeguard investors who make high-risk or alternative investments.

The requirements that an investor must meet before qualifying for EIS income tax relief are contained within Chapter 2 of Part 5 of ITA 2007. All references given below are therefore to this statute, unless otherwise stated. Before looking at the conditions in detail, it is worthwhile spending some time becoming familiar with the various periods and dates referred to in the legislation, as these are referred to frequently throughout.

The investor needs to be an individual, but there is no requirement that he must be UK resident or domiciled. He would, however, need a UK income tax liability to take advantage of the income tax relief. Trustees cannot claim the income tax relief, though the beneficiary of a bare trust or nominee arrangement could.

Some of the conditions related to the individual are relaxed when looking at CGT deferral relief, which we will discuss later on.

Law: ITA 2007, s. 157

2.2 Periods and key dates

2.2.1 Periods A, B and C

Some of the qualifying conditions need to be met only at the time of investment; however, some need to be met for periods beginning before the investment date, and/or afterwards.

This can be confusing, but the legislation helpfully defines three key periods in order to help avoid confusion. These are:

1. Period A – beginning with either the incorporation date, or two years before the share issue date (whichever is later), and ending immediately before the "termination date" of the relevant shares (see **2.2.2** below).
2. Period B – beginning with the share issue date, and ending immediately before the termination date.
3. Period C – beginning 12 months before the share issue, and ending immediately before the termination date.

In particular it is important to recognise the difference between Period A and Period B, and to be clear which "relevant period" is being referred to when using the legislation.

Law: ITA 2007, s. 159

2.2.2 Termination date

In practice the termination date relating to relevant shares is the date when all the relief becomes final – i.e., if all the qualifying conditions have been met throughout the period leading up to this date, there is no longer a risk that this might be withdrawn.

Exactly when the termination date is depends on whether the company was already carrying on the qualifying trade at the time the shares were issued. If it was, the termination date will be the third anniversary of the share issue date. As this is the case with most EIS investments, there is often confusion and an incorrect assumption that the termination date is always three years after the shares were subscribed for. There are instances, however, where this will not be the case.

If the company invested in have not yet commenced carrying on the qualifying trade but is preparing to do so, the termination date will be the third anniversary of the date that trade commences. This preparation work can continue for up to two years after the share issue date (discussed in a later chapter) without jeopardising EIS relief. The termination date can therefore potentially be up to five years after the share issue date where this is applicable.

If an investor makes a disposal of some or all of the shares before the termination date, the relief given will be fully or partially withdrawn, depending on the circumstances.

Law: ITA 2007, s. 256

2.2.3 Share issue date

It has been established by case law that the shares are treated as issued once the investor is legally entitled to them. In practice this means when he is entitled to exercise his voting rights, receive dividends, etc. This will be effective once the relevant entries are written into the register of members. Whilst this will often be the same day the shares are paid for and the corresponding certificate is issued to the new shareholders, this is not necessarily always the case.

If there is a delay in making the relevant entries, then the termination date may actually be later than thought. This could be a problem if the shareholder then sells the shares after the third anniversary of paying for them, but before the third anniversary of the entries actually being made in the register. This could prove very costly, so investors should be sure to enquire as to when the entries are made.

Guidance: VCM 12020

2.3 Conditions for the investor

2.3.1 Overview

There are three main qualifying conditions that an investor must meet to obtain EIS relief:

1. he or she must not be connected to, or become connected to, the issuing company at any time during Period A;
2. there must be no linked loans in relation to the investment during Period A;

3. the investment must be made for a genuine commercial purpose, and not as part of tax avoidance scheme.

In addition to these, *Finance (No. 2) Act* 2015 introduced rules applicable to existing shareholders which are considered at **2.3.9** below.

Law: ITA 2007, s. 162

2.3.2 Connections – introduction

A person is considered to be connected with the issuing company in three circumstances, namely:

1. where he or she is an employee, director or partner;
2. where his or her interest in the company's capital exceeds the permitted amount; or
3. where shares are subscribed for under certain arrangements.

We will consider each of these in turn.

Remember that when looking at whether a connection exists, the relevant period is Period A – that is the period beginning two years prior to the share issue, and ending immediately before the termination date. Any connection preceding or following that time period can be ignored for these purposes.

It is also important to note that an individual will be treated as connected where he does not himself have a connection, but where an associate of his does have.

An associate for these purposes includes a spouse or civil partner, a parent or another linear ancestor (for example, a grandparent), or a natural child and other linear descendants (for example, grandchildren).

Associates will also include a business partner (that is to say someone the individual carries on business with in a partnership) and any trustee of a settlement the individual has made.

Law: ITA 2007, s. 163, 166, 253

2.3.3 Connections – employees, etc.

If the investor is, at any time during the relevant period, an employee (or director) of:

- the issuing company or one of its subsidiaries;
- a partner of the issuing company; or
- a subsidiary of a partner of the issuing company,

then the condition set out in s. 157(1) – namely that the individual must be a qualifying investor – is not met. There are special provisions regarding directors that can give an exception to this general rule, and we will consider this at **2.3.4** below.

The term "partner" here is meant in its business sense – that is to say two companies that are corporate partners in a partnership. So if the individual is an employee of A Ltd, which is a corporate partner in AB LLP along with B Ltd, the individual would be precluded from EIS relief on any investment into B Ltd.

Law: ITA 2007, s. 157(1)

2.3.4 Connections – directors

The position relating to directors is complicated, and often misunderstood by advisers and investors alike. There is a predisposition to assume that, provided the investor is a director of the company rather than simply an employee, the exemptions mentioned at **2.3.3** above apply automatically, and EIS relief can be claimed on investment.

This is fundamentally incorrect and, if not properly understood, could lead to a loss or denial of relief. Consider, for example, an employee who becomes a director a week before the investment that is intended to qualify. The special provisions relating to directors will not apply because there has already been a connection (as an employee) during Period A. If an individual has been an employee at any time in the two years prior to the share issue date, simply becoming a director will not displace the connection.

There are two exemptions relating to directors. The first is for unpaid directors, and the second is for paid "business angel" type investor-directors. These are contained within sections 168 and 169 respectively.

Unpaid directors

This exemption allows a director to be considered a qualifying investor if the individual does not receive payment, or become entitled to a payment, other than those permitted by s. 168. Broadly this prohibits a salary from being paid, but allows payments that would ordinarily be expected to be reimbursed to an individual acting in his capacity as a director (or indeed shareholder).

Examples of such non-disqualifying payments include:

- any business expenses that would qualify for a deduction under ITEPA 2003, s. 336 – i.e. expenses incurred wholly, exclusively and necessarily in the performance of the employment duties;
- dividends paid at a commercial rate;
- interest on any loans which is paid at a commercial rate; and
- reasonable rent paid for any property owned by the individual and used by the issuing company – provided this is equivalent to an arm's-length rate.

There is also a narrowly defined tolerance for payments made to the individual in respect of services provided to the issuing company (or related party), where these payments constitute trading or professional income which will be accountable to tax.

If these conditions are satisfied, and the individual was not an employee without also being a director at any time during Period A, the director is not precluded from claiming EIS relief.

Paid directors

A further, more powerful, exception is contained in s. 169. This is a separate provision from the one described above, and allows so-called business angel investors to become paid directors, provided that their remuneration is not excessive. The term "business angel" is not defined in the tax legislation, but is understood to mean an investor who wishes to provide experience and expertise in addition to financial investment.

Provided that any remuneration is reasonable in respect of the services the investor provides to the company, such directors can qualify for EIS relief provided they have never been:

- connected with the company; or
- involved in carrying on any part of the trade or business of the company or one of its subsidiaries.

Not meeting these two requirements may not be fatal to an EIS claim if there has been a previous eligible share issue under either EIS or SEIS, and the two requirements were satisfied at the time of that earlier issue - provided the termination date related to those shares has not yet passed.

If there is no previous share issue, and the two requirements are not satisfied, a paid director cannot claim EIS relief.

Involved in carrying on the trade?

In most cases, it would be prudent to delay appointing an investor as a director until after the share issue date, even if no remuneration is to be paid. This is because an appointment prior to this date may lead to HMRC trying to deny relief on the grounds that the director was involved in carrying on part of the trade or business of the company. This could potentially be difficult to disprove - particularly if the individual has already attended meetings, etc.

An important distinction here is that to fail the test, the director has to be shown to be involved in the trade or business of the company. If the company has not yet commenced trading, and the EIS relief is therefore relying on the condition of preparing to carry out a qualifying trade, this should not be a problem. This was established in *Thomason & Ors*, which also considered the eligibility of a director who was a director of the company previously carrying on a trade but subsequently acquired by the issuing company. The test is therefore only applicable in the context of whether the director has ever been involved with carrying on the trade in so far as it relates to the issuing company, rather than the trade itself.

Law: ITA 2007, s. 168, 169

Case: *Thomason & Ors v HMRC* [2010] UKFTT 579 (TC)

2.3.5 Connections – substantial interest

An individual will be considered connected to the issuing company if, during Period A, he (alone or together with his associates) directly or indirectly owns or becomes entitled to acquire more than 30% of:

- the ordinary share capital;
- the voting rights; or
- the rights to assets upon a winding up,

in respect of the issuing company.

The presence of the term "indirectly" here prevents an individual from keeping his own interests below the stipulated amounts, whilst concurrently owning additional interests via (say) a company which he controls, or through a trust of which he is the main beneficiary.

In respect of the 30% test, this is not applied in the situation where the initial shareholdings upon incorporation would lead to the threshold being exceeded – i.e. subscriber shares and shareholding ratios are essentially ignored during the period prior to when the company first begins to prepare to carry on the trade.

Example – substantial interest

Bob and Bill form a company together holding one share each on incorporation. The company does not carry on a trade initially; however, after a month the company issues shares to various EIS investors, and these funds are used to acquire a trade from another company. Following the new share issues, Bob and Bill own 15% each. Despite the fact that during Period A they owned 50% each, this can be disregarded provided no other changes were made to the share capital prior to the qualifying share issue.

Law: ITA 2007, s. 170

2.3.6 Connections – arrangements

There will be a deemed connection in some circumstances. The anti-avoidance provision in s. 171 prevents otherwise non-qualifying individuals from obtaining relief by using so-called reciprocal arrangements.

Consider the following scenario:

Example – arrangements

Andy and Pete both run their own companies. They wish to put £100,000 each into these respective companies to increase working capital, as they both have large projects coming up. Pete has the ingenious idea that rather than putting money into their own companies, they both invest in one another's – i.e. Pete puts £100,000 into Andy's company, and vice versa. The end result for the companies is the same; however Pete thinks this means that both he and Andy can claim £30,000 of EIS relief.

Section 171 prevents the above scenario from working. It is not restricted to reciprocal arrangements, and broadly prevents individuals from trying to circumvent the connected persons test.

Law: ITA 2007, s. 171

2.3.7 Linked loans

Relief is not available if, during Period A, the investor receives a loan which in the absence of an investment:

- would not have been made; or
- would not have been made on the same terms.

In most uncomplicated situations (e.g. an outside investor funding a new company), this is unlikely to present a problem when looking directly at the investor-company relationship. This is because a company seeking to raise capital for a qualifying purpose would not be in a position to be making loans in the first place. The provision is rather intended to catch out schemes or arrangements where the investor essentially gets his money straight back, obtaining a valuable relief with little or no reduction in his or her capital.

This provision does not just apply to loans made from the issuing company (or any of its subsidiaries), however. Any loan that can be linked to the shares issued will fall foul of the rules, where this would not have been made – or would not have been made on the same terms – without the investment taking place.

To illustrate how this might apply in practice, consider the following example.

Example – linked loans

Margaret wants to invest in her friend's textile manufacturing company. She wishes to invest £200,000 under EIS, but does not have cash assets. She approaches her bank for a loan, disclosing the purpose in full. The bank agrees to make the loan but insists on taking a charge over the shares in the company as collateral. Because this loan is directly linked to the shares (because of the charge), it is a linked loan, and precludes Margaret from claiming EIS relief.

Section 164 extends the meaning of loan for these purposes to include the extension of credit to the investor (or his associates), and assignment of debts due from the investor (or his associates).

Law: ITA 2007, s. 164

2.3.8 Commercial reasoning

In order for an investment to qualify for EIS relief, it has to be made for a genuine commercial purpose – even if no connection exists. The test is subjective, and so is hard to measure or prove; however HMRC guidance does point to certain situations it deems would not be considered commercial. One is where the main motivation for making the investment is benevolence – e.g. putting money into an obviously failing company because of sentimental ties. Another would be an investment made by a terminally ill person, as there is no realistic probability of a return to that person.

Similarly, there is a general exclusion for investments where the main purpose, or one of the main purposes, of making the investment is the avoidance of tax. It is not thought that simply seeking to access the tax relief itself would constitute avoidance – and so investors do not have to be able to prove that they would have made the investment regardless of the EIS relief. This is confirmed by HMRC. HMRC also confirm that, in their opinion, tax avoidance will be a factor in situations where relief has been obtained in circumstances that Parliament did not intend.

Law: ITA 2007, s. 165
Guidance: VCM 11040

2.3.9 Existing shareholders

From 18 November 2015 a new condition was introduced, adding a further restrict to the availability of EIS relief to existing shareholders. For share issues on or after that date, any individual holding shares in either:

- the issuing company; or
- a company which is a qualifying subsidiary at the share issue date,

can only obtain EIS relief on an investment for further shares if the existing shares:

- were issued as a risk finance investment (namely one for which EIS, SEIS, or Social Investment Tax Relief (SITR) was given); or
- are subscriber shares (i.e. shares in existence when the company was originally formed) which the individual:
    - has held since throughout, and
    - subscribed for at a time when the company had only issued subscriber shares, and had not begun to carry on a trade or preparatory work intended to lead to a trade.

Law: ITA 2007, s. 164A

3. Income tax relief: company conditions

3.1 Introduction

In order for a share issue to qualify under EIS, it must be made by a "qualifying company". Both the legislation and HMRC guidance make frequent reference to this term.

Conditions are set by the legislation ensuring that only smaller, newer, and generally riskier companies are able to access capital via EIS – as Parliament intended initially. In recent years new criteria have been introduced to restrict what kind of trade a qualifying company can carry out. There have also been restrictions levied on the age of the company, and the amount of risk capital finance (including EIS) it can raise. Most of these restrictions have been imposed to ensure that EIS continues to receive EU State aid approval.

Law: ITA 2007, s. 180

3.2 Conditions to be met by the issuing company

3.2.1 Overview

Section 180 neatly summarises all of the conditions which are pertinent to the issuing company. As mentioned above, the legislation and HMRC guidance make frequent reference to a "qualifying company". The company is only be qualifying if it meets all of the conditions listed in s. 180, which relate to:

- UK permanent establishment;
- financial health;
- trading and qualifying trade;
- unquoted status;
- control and independence;
- gross assets;
- number of employees;
- qualifying subsidiaries; and
- property management subsidiaries.

Some of these tests are purely qualitative, and therefore easy to measure – such as the number of employees. Others have a more subjective nature, and therefore judgements must sometimes be exercised, with reliance on case law in some circumstances.

As we saw with the investor, some of the conditions have to be met only at the time of the investment, whereas others must be met for a period of time afterwards as well. Having conditions which are only assessed at the time of investment demonstrates that EIS is intended to help entrepreneurial businesses grow. It would be counter-productive to the UK economy, for example, to encourage investment in smaller companies, only to remove any incentives to do so if such companies are then successful and want to float on the stock exchange.

Law: ITA 2007, s. 180

3.2.2 UK permanent establishment

A company cannot be a qualifying company for the purposes of EIS unless it has a permanent establishment in the UK. Section 191A provides that the company will have a UK permanent establishment if one of the following two conditions is met:

- it has a fixed place of business in the UK through which the company's business is wholly or partly carried on; or
- an agent acting on behalf the company has habitually exercised its authority to enter into contracts on behalf of the company.

The most obvious way to qualify is therefore to have a physical presence – i.e. an office building located in the UK from which at least some of the business operates. HMRC guidance in the *Venture Capital Schemes Manual* includes an illustrative list of what they consider to be a fixed place of business:

> "The legislation lists a number of examples, including:
>
> - a place of management;
> - a branch;
> - an office;
> - a factory,
> - a workshop,

- a mine, oil or gas well,
- a quarry or any other place of extraction of natural resources; and
- a building site or construction or installation project.

This list is not intended to be exhaustive; the type of business will determine the type and nature of the premises or facilities required."

If the permanent establishment test cannot be met using the fixed place of business condition, the agent condition can be looked at as an alternative. Here it is key that the agent or agents have authority to enter into contracts as if they were the company itself. A mere employee who would require approval or sign off to enter into a binding contract on behalf the company would be unlikely to meet this condition. The type of contracts the agent is authorised to enter into must also be substantial enough to constitute matters central to the company business, not merely auxiliary services.

In most cases, prospective EIS qualifying companies will be UK companies anyway. Prior to April 2011, in order to qualify the company had to carry on its business wholly or mainly in the UK. This was a far more restrictive condition designed to prevent investment partly funded by UK tax relief flowing outside of the UK.

Following this law change it is perfectly possible for a qualifying investment to be made in a non-UK company, provided it has either a fixed place of business or an agent in the UK. Remember, however, that the condition applies to the issuing company, and so an overseas registered parent company will not automatically meet the condition simply because it has a UK subsidiary – it must meet the condition in its own right. The subsidiary itself cannot be the issuing company because of the control independence requirement (discussed at **3.2.7** below).

Law: ITA 2007, s. 180A, 191A
Guidance: VCM 13030

3.2.3 Financial health

The company cannot be a qualifying company if, on the date the shares are issued, it is considered to be "in difficulty" as defined by EC guidelines on State aid.

Whether a company is in difficulty for these purposes may be difficult to determine precisely. The guidelines are lengthy; however, a certain amount of common sense and professional opinion should give a feel for the overall health of the company. If there are large losses, high leverage, debts, falling customer numbers, a low or negative balance sheet value, the signs are there that there is at least a question to be asked. That question may be "is this company realistically able to continue operating as a going concern using its own resources, and without outside assistance in the short to medium term?".

HMRC reproduce what they see as the most relevant paragraphs from the EC guidelines at VCM 13040.

The company will not be regarded as being in difficulty if it is newly created – that is to say it is still within its first three years of operations. This is particularly useful for many R&D type companies that are still working to bring a saleable product to market.

Law: ITA 2007, s. 180B
Guidance: VCM 13040

3.2.4 Trading

The issuing company cannot be a qualifying company unless it exists wholly for the purpose of carrying on one or more qualifying trades or, alternatively, it is the parent company of a trading group when looking at the group activities as a whole. This condition has to be met from the date of issue of the shares through to the termination date – i.e. throughout Period B.

The condition can be viewed as a test of intention, and so the fact that – at the time of the share issue – the trade intended to take place has not yet commenced in the newly formed company should not be fatal to meeting the qualifying company condition. Things may become more complicated if funds held on account are invested into relatively illiquid assets, even if it is intended to realise these for the purposes of commencing trading later on. Simply holding cash on deposit, however, should not pose a problem unless the delay becomes substantial. In practice HMRC will look at what the directors actually do, rather than what the original stated intention may have been when considering what the company really exists for.

A single company will be considered to be trading if it does not carry on non-qualifying activities other than up to an incidental level. Earning interest on cash held on deposit therefore should not preclude such a company from qualifying; however if investment income from various sources forms a substantial part of the company's business turnover it is likely to fail this test. Note that due to the wording of the provision, the non-qualifying activity need not be substantial, merely more than incidental.

If the issuing company is the parent company of a group, it is the activity of the group taken together as a whole that must be considered when looking at non-qualifying activities. This provision is worded slightly differently so that the parent company will only fail the test if the group's non-qualifying activities are substantial. Substantial is taken to mean more than 20%, and should be measured by reference to factors such as turnover, cost overheads, employee and management time commitment, and the employment of assets.

This can lead to a parent company whose group has non-qualifying activities being a qualifying company, where a single company with the same mix of qualifying and non-qualifying activities would fail.

Example – advantage of group structure

A Ltd is a single company which has 85% trading activities, and 15% rental investment activities. B Ltd is the parent company of B group. Its only subsidiary is wholly owned and has exactly the same mix of activities as A Ltd. B Ltd could potentially qualify under EIS; however A Ltd could not, as 15% is clearly more than incidental.

This could be viewed as an unfair result given that – other than the corporate structure, which is essentially a paper exercise – the underlying activities are identical. If it is thought that this is going to be a problem, the possibility of restructuring an existing single company into a two company group ahead of the investment date can be explored. Remember that the condition only has to be met throughout Period B, which starts with the date of the share issue, so provided the restructuring is done before the issue date, there will be no breach of the condition.

The meaning of "qualifying trade" is considered below.

Law: ITA 2007, s. 181-182

3.2.5 Qualifying trade

For a company to be considered to be carrying on a qualifying trade for EIS purposes, it must be operating its trade on a commercial basis with a view to the realisation of profits. Again this is a partly subjective test, at least for newly formed companies as there may not be enough financial information to reach a conclusion as to the commerciality of trade yet. There is a general condition (discussed in the next chapter) that the money raised through an EIS investment must be used for the purposes of a qualifying business activity. A qualifying business activity will either constitute a qualifying trade, or preparatory work intended to lead to the commencement of a qualifying trade, either carried out (or intended to be carried out) by the issuing company or by a qualifying 90% subsidiary thereof. As will be seen, ultimately no EIS relief can be given in the absence of a qualifying trade, and so we must consider what this is.

If a company is preparing to commence a qualifying trade, EIS relief can be granted on issue of the shares; however the qualifying trade must then commence within two years of the share issue date or the relief will be withdrawn. Note that this can mean that the termination date of the shares is up to five years from issue, as the three year holding period commences when the trade commences if it has not done so at the time of the share issue.

If a company is undertaking research and development intended to lead to the commencement of a qualifying trade, EIS relief can be granted on issue of the shares; however, preliminary work – such as market research to determine whether the trade is likely to succeed – will not count as research and development for this purpose.

Additionally, there are a number of specified excluded activities which could prevent a company from being a qualifying company, if such activities are substantial. Note that this is slightly different from the test in the section above because some of the specified excluded activities are actually trades themselves. Again substantial is given to mean 20%.

Broadly, any trade will be qualifying unless it is specifically excluded by the legislation. At the time of writing, the list of excluded activities given by s. 192 is as follows:

- Dealing in goods otherwise than in the course of an ordinary trade of wholesale or retail distribution.
- Banking, insurance, money-lending, debt-factoring, hire-purchase financing or other financial activities.
- Leasing (including letting ships on charter or other assets on hire).
- Receiving royalties or licence fees.
- Providing legal or accountancy services.
- Property development.
- Farming or market gardening.
- Holding, managing or occupying woodlands, any other forestry activities or timber production.
- Shipbuilding.
- Producing coal.
- Producing steel.
- Operating or managing hotels or comparable establishments.
- Operating or managing nursing homes or residential care homes.
- Generating or exporting electricity or making electricity generating capacity available.
- Generating heat.
- Generating any form of energy not within the above two points.
- Producing gas or fuel.
- Provision of services or facilities for another business.

Financial activities relate solely to dealing in financial products in one form or another. It is perfectly possible, therefore, for an independent financial adviser to form a limited company and to seek investment by EIS – subject to the usual restrictions regarding insubstantial non-qualifying activities.

Until recently, it was possible to set up a company to receive investment by EIS where in reality its only source of income consisted of government subsidies for renewable energy generation. For example, the renewable heating incentive provided guaranteed income for 20 years to the owner of approved generation equipment. A company could take a limited lease of a small part of a large building, say a nursing home, install the equipment (on its own premises technically), and pay for the lease by providing the nursing home with cheap or even free electricity. As the incentive payments were based on usage, this could be extremely profitable, and virtually risk-free as the income was guaranteed by the government. HMRC's arguments that an excluded activity (leasing) was taking place were refuted because ownership of the equipment was never surrendered by the issuing company. This was key because the renewable heating incentive payments had to be made to the legal owner – including a lessee – of the biomass technology.

Clearly this type of contrived arrangement (which not only virtually guaranteed no risk for investors, but also allowed a healthy income to be paid) is not in keeping with the intentions of Parliament when it introduced EIS, and it is unsurprising that it was quickly shut down.

Receivership/winding up

Because the trading conditions need to be satisfied throughout Period B, it is entirely possible that despite the best endeavours of the directors, the company's business simply fails. If the trade ceases because the company is placed into administration or receivership, or a petition is made for its winding up, the company will not be treated as having breached the trading conditions, provided the action was taken for genuine commercial reasons. HMRC confirm that if the company ceases the trade because of an expected liquidation, then the sooner the liquidation actually happens following the cessation the more likely it is that relief will not be withdrawn, as it can be established that there will be no return to the investor.

Law: ITA 2007, s. 181, 183, 192
Guidance: VCM 13070

3.2.6 Unquoted status

This condition is relatively easy to measure. At the time of the investment, the issuing company must be unquoted – that is to say its shares must not be listed on a recognised stock exchange. AIM listed shares are treated as unquoted for these purposes. HMRC guidance also stipulates that some of the PLUS markets were also treated as unquoted; however this is now defunct. PLUS was acquired by ICAP in 2012, and it would appear that its small entrepreneurial markets – e.g. ISDX growth – are also treated as unquoted.

As well as meeting this condition at the time of investment, there must be no existing arrangements for the company to become quoted, or to become a subsidiary of another company which is quoted (or will become quoted as a result of existing arrangements).

Note that these conditions do not prevent the issuing company from becoming successful within Period B and securing quoted status due to that success. In that scenario relief would not be withdrawn.

Law: ITA 2007, s. 184

3.2.7 Control and independence

Again the period under scrutiny here is Period B.

At no point during this period may the issuing company (alone or with any connected persons) control any subsidiaries which are not "qualifying subsidiaries". A qualifying subsidiary is one of which the issuing company directly or indirectly holds more than 50% of the ordinary share capital, and no other person other than the relevant company or its subsidiaries has control of it.

Additionally, the issuing company must be independent; that is to say it must not itself be under the control of another company – whether alone or with any persons connected to that company. Basically if the issuing company is part of a group, it needs to be the top company.

Law: ITA 2007, s. 185

3.2.8 Gross assets

This test is applicable at the time of the share issue.

The gross assets of the company (or amalgamated gross assets of group companies) must not exceed:

- £15 million immediately before the relevant investment; or

- £16 million immediately after the relevant investment.

Gross assets refer to the value (before deducting any liabilities) of any property the company owns that would appear on the balance sheet were it to draw one up on the investment date. The valuation method cannot be altered from that used to prepare the most recent financial statements – so an artificially depressed value cannot be achieved through (say) a change in depreciation policy.

HMRC guidance confirms that any cash received as an advance toward the investment (i.e. conditionally for and in expectation of the share issue) will not be considered to form part of the gross assets.

In the case of groups, any intra-company balances such as loans, or the value of intra-group shareholdings, are disregarded.

If a company meets the pre-investment condition, it should be recalled that the post-investment limit could serve to restrict the amount that can be raised under EIS.

Law: ITA 2007, s. 186
Guidance: VCM 13110

3.2.9 Number of employees

At the time of the investment, the issuing company (or group as a whole) must have fewer than 250 full time equivalent employees (including directors). From 18 November 2015, this limit is increased to 500 if the company qualifies as a "knowledge-intensive company" (see **3.3** below).

Full time for this purpose means an employee who normally works at least 35 hours per week.

Part time employees need to be accounted for, and in doing so their hours need to be aggregated together. For example, two employees who both work 17.5 hours per week together constitute one single full time equivalent for the purpose of the limit.

Only employees who are still working for the company at the issue date need to be accounted for – so seasonal staff may not need to be counted.

Law: ITA 2007, s. 186A

3.2.10 Qualifying subsidiaries

There is a specific condition that if the issuing company has any subsidiaries during Period B, they must be qualifying subsidiaries as discussed above at **3.2.7**.

Law: ITA 2007, s. 187

3.2.11 Property management subsidiaries

An extension to the general condition regarding qualifying subsidiaries is that, if any of the company's subsidiaries carries on a business which is mainly that of holding land or property deriving value from land, that subsidiary has to be a 90% subsidiary (rather than just a 51% subsidiary).

Of course the overall impact of the non-qualifying activity would also need to be reviewed to determine whether it is "substantial".

Law: ITA 2007, s. 188

3.3 Meaning of knowledge-intensive company

A knowledge-intensive company is a company:

- whose costs of research and development or innovation are at least 15% of the company's operating costs in at least one of the previous 3 years, or at least 10% of the company's operating costs in each of the previous 3 years and either:
    - the company has created, is creating or is intending to create, intellectual property, or
    - the company's employees with a relevant Masters or higher degree who are engaged in research and development or innovation comprise at least 20% of the company's total workforce.

If the shares are issued in the first three years that the company is trading, the operating costs conditions above are measured by the three years following the investment instead.

Law: ITA 2007, s. 252A

4. Income tax relief: general requirements

4.1 Introduction

In addition to the specific requirements to be met by the investor and the issuing company, there are a number of conditions which are grouped together in the legislation under the heading "general requirements". These conditions relate to the nature of the investment itself; however, confusingly new conditions introduced by F(No. 2)A 2015 (which appear to relate directly to the issuing company) have been included under this heading as well.

It is worth noting at the outset that the issuing company itself has to carry on the qualifying activity, unless the activities are carried out by a qualifying 90% subsidiary. There is, however, no requirement that a 90% subsidiary needs to be UK resident, and so shares could be issued by a UK parent company with the funds raised diverted entirely offshore.

Law: ITA 2007, s. 183

4.2 General requirements

4.2.1 Overview

The conditions set out by the legislation are those related to:

- the shares;
- maximum risk finance investments (annual);
- maximum risk finance investments (lifetime);
- purpose of the issue;
- use of the money;
- permitted maximum age;
- minimum period;
- pre-arranged exits;
- tax avoidance; and
- disqualifying arrangements.

We will consider each of these in turn.

Law: ITA 2007, s. 172

4.2.2 The shares

In order to qualify for EIS relief, the shares issued must form part of the ordinary share capital of the company, with no present or future preferential rights in respect of dividends, redemption, or to the company's assets upon a winding up, for the entirety of Period B. The purpose of this restriction is to ensure that investors are participating in the company on a full risk basis.

It is often the case in practice that EIS shares are issued under a separate class – e.g. B shares. The restriction does not prevent separate dividends being voted to the holders of the EIS shares in this case, provided the shares carry the same rights to dividends as other classes of shares.

Ordinary share capital is defined by s. 989 as:

> "... in relation to a company, means all the company's issued share capital (however described), other than the capital the holders of which have a right to a dividend at a fixed rate, but have no other right to share in the company's profits."

Unless the shares are bonus shares, they must also be fully paid up in cash at the time of the issue. Any delay in transferring money to pay for the shares could lead to HMRC challenging a claim to EIS relief on the basis that this condition was not met, as it did with some success in *Blackburn*.

It is clear that for a share issue to qualify for EIS some money has to change hands. The conversion of loan notes into shares (in satisfaction of the debt on the notes) was held not to be a subscription for shares in *Optos*.

Law: ITA 2007, s. 173

Cases: *Optos plc v R&C Commrs* (2006) Sp C 560; *Blackburn & Another v R&C Commrs* (2007) Sp C 606

4.2.3 Maximum amount raised via risk finance investments (annual)

An annual investment limit for "relevant investments" was introduced in 2007, and has gradually increased over time to its current limit of £5 million.

The investment is a relevant investment if it was made under EIS or SEIS, or if it qualified for Social Investment Tax Relief (SITR). Relevant investments also include certain grants or subsidies from governments: these have the hallmarks of State aid as set out by the European Commission.

The limit is not applicable by reference to the tax year but rather is a rolling 12-month limit, so you need to look for any investments made in the 12 months prior to the prospective share issue date. It should be noted that if an investment means that the limit is breached, the whole amount of it will fail to qualify for EIS relief – not just the excess above the limit.

Finance Act 2018 contained legislation to increase this limit to £10 million for knowledge-intensive companies only (see **3.3**).

Law: ITA 2007, s. 173A

4.2.4 Maximum amount raised via risk finance investments (lifetime)

Finance (No. 2) Act 2015 introduced an additional limit on monies raised via relevant investments. There are actually two provisions relating to this.

The first is measured at the share issue date, and stipulates that the maximum relevant investments the company can have received on or before that date is £12 million. This limit is increased to £20 million if the company qualifies as "knowledge-intensive" (see **3.3**).

The second provision is virtually identical; however, it extends the requirement not to exceed this investment limit for the duration of Period B. This means the shares could initially attract EIS relief, but have this removed if further investment is received, or if certain grants or subsidies are received.

Note that any relevant investments into subsidiary companies must be taken into account when looking at these limits.

Investments will only be relevant investments if a compliance statement was actually issued under the relevant legislation, so a large investment for which EIS relief (or otherwise) was refused will not count for these purposes.

Finance Act 2018 made changes to ensure that all investments received under EIS, SEIS, VCT or SITR count as "relevant" investments for the purpose of the limit.

Law: ITA 2007, s. 173AA, 173AB

4.2.5 Purpose of the issue

The shares must be issued in order to raise money to fund a qualifying activity, so as to promote business growth and development. Again referring to the decision in *Optos*, converting the loan notes into shares did not raise any cash to the business although it may have released a debt and so would have failed this condition as well.

Similarly, raising money in order to pay dividends to shareholders was held not to meet this condition in *Forthright (Wales) Ltd.*

Law: ITA 2007, s. 174

Cases: *Forthright (Wales) Ltd v Davies* (2004) 76 TC 138; *Optos plc v R&C Commrs* (2006) Sp C 560

4.2.6 Use of the money

The money raised by the share issue has to be employed for a qualifying purpose by the later of:

- two years from the issue of the shares; or
- two years from the date on which the company begins to carry on a qualifying trade – if the original qualifying activity was preparing to do so.

Relief will not be lost if an amount of the money raised which is not significant is not so employed. Exactly what constitutes "significant" for these purposes is unclear, and will probably need to be reviewed in light of the total amount raised. An unemployed amount of £10,000 is far more likely to be accepted as not significant if the amount raised was £5 million rather than £100,000.

Section 175 specifically excludes certain things from being a qualifying purpose, namely using the funds directly or indirectly to acquire:

- a majority interest in another company;
- a further interest in a company which is already a subsidiary;
- a trade;
- intangible assets employed for the purposes of the trade; or
- goodwill employed for the purposes of the trade.

The requirement for the money to be employed, rather than simply spent or extinguished means that in certain limited circumstances, monies can be said considered to be employed even though they have not been spent. For this to apply they would have to be earmarked with sufficient certainty and purpose toward a future event – for example a business expansion. This was established in *Skye Inns Ltd.*

Law: ITA 2007, s. 175

Case: *Skye Inns Ltd and Mr Chris Richards v HMRC* [2009] UKFTT 366 (TC)

4.2.7 Maximum permitted age

This provision identifies an initial eligible investing period which is seven years from the date of the first commercial sale – unless the company is a "knowledge-intensive company" (see **3.3**), in which case this is increased to ten years.

If an investment is made after this initial investing period, it can only qualify under EIS if one of three conditions is met.

> Condition A: the new investment is a follow-on investment to one which qualified for EIS within the initial investing period, and some or all of that money raised was used for a qualifying purpose.
>
> Condition B: the amount raised under relevant investments over a 30 day period (including the issue date) is equal to at least half of the average turnover (over the previous five years), and this money is used for the purposes of entering a new product or geographical market.

Condition C: condition B was met in respect of the previous share issue, and some or all of the money raised under that share issue was used for a qualifying purpose.

The restriction serves to ensure that EIS is only available to newer companies, or those that are looking to make a drastic change to the nature of their trade or the base of their operations.

Following the enactment of FA 2018, it is possible for a knowledge-intensive company to elect to measure its age from the date that it is treated as reaching an annual turnover of £200,000 instead of the date of the first commercial sale. The date is treated as being the last day of the first accounting period where the turnover exceeds £200,000.

Law: ITA 2007, s. 175A

4.2.8 Minimum period

No relief can be granted until the qualifying activity, whether that be the qualifying trade or the preparatory work intended to lead to one, has been carried out for at least four months. In practice this simply delays a brand-new company, which receives investment upon incorporation, from applying for a compliance statement for four months.

Law: ITA 2007, s. 176

4.2.9 Pre-arranged exits

Relief will be denied on any shares issued under arrangements which would effectively guarantee (or at least make it likely) that the investor will receive his or her money back at some point in the future through some mechanism.

Arrangements caught by this provision are set out in s. 177:

"(a) arrangements with a view to the subsequent repurchase, exchange or other disposal of those shares or of other shares in or securities of the issuing company,

(b) arrangements for or with a view to the cessation of any trade which is being or is to be or may be carried on by the issuing company or a person connected with that company,

(c) arrangements for the disposal of, or of a substantial amount (in terms of value) of, the assets of the issuing company or of a person connected with that company, or

(d) arrangements the main purpose or one of the main purposes of which is (by means of any insurance, indemnity or guarantee or otherwise) to provide partial or complete protection for persons investing in shares in the issuing company against what would otherwise be the risks attached to making the investment."

The most straightforward arrangements which might be seen (or at least suggested) in practice would be an undertaking on behalf of the company to repurchase the shares at purchase price after the termination date provided a success hurdle is met. The idea is that the investor banks the tax relief, then gets back the cash used to make the investment. This would be sufficient to disqualify the investment from EIS.

HMRC do make clear that there is nothing wrong with a company indicating to potential investors how they feel that the value in the shares may be realised at some later date – as of course genuine investors will be seeking to make a return on the investment.

There are limited circumstances – broadly those which would be undertaken in the ordinary course of a trade – where relief would not be denied or removed:

- certain takeovers which occur under very narrowly drawn circumstances;
- arrangements which ensure the company could be wound up in an orderly manner should the need arise for genuine commercial reasons; and
- the company being an indemnified or protected party under (for example) public liability insurance policies.

A clause containing the right to convert shares from one class to another will not prevent relief from being issued; however, any conversion must take place after the termination date.

Law: ITA 2007, s. 177

4.2.10 Tax avoidance

As with most government endorsed tax reliefs, relief cannot be given unless the transaction is entered into for a genuine commercial purpose, and not as part of a scheme or arrangement, the main purpose (or one of the main purposes) of which is the avoidance of tax.

HMRC confirm that simply making an investment with the aim of it qualifying for EIS relief (as opposed to one which clearly would not) will not be viewed as tax avoidance.

Law: ITA 2007, s. 178
Guidance: VCM 12090

4.2.11 Disqualifying arrangements

The concept of disqualifying arrangements was introduced for share issues after April 2012. If the shares are issued under arrangements which are "disqualifying", no relief can be attributed to them.

Arrangements will be disqualifying if either condition A or B is met.

Condition A is that as a result (direct or indirect) of the money raised by the share issue, all or most of that money (or an equivalent amount) is subsequently paid to or for the benefit of a relevant person or persons.

A relevant person is one who is party to the arrangements, or someone connected to such a person.

Example

Bill invests £1 million in Mark's company, A Ltd. Shortly afterwards, A Ltd spends £900,000 on marketing services provided by B Ltd – a company wholly owned by Bill's wife. This would appear to fall foul of the disqualifying arrangement provision under Condition A.

Condition B is applicable in circumstances where, in the absence of the arrangements, it would have been reasonable to expect that the whole or greater part of the component activities of the relevant business activity would have been carried on as part of another business by a person or by persons who are party to the arrangements or a person or persons connected with such a party.

This appears to prevent situations where an otherwise non-qualifying entity wishes to start a new venture, and does so through a newly formed company owned and run by others, for the sole reason that EIS relief would not otherwise be available.

HMRC's guidance indicates that the purpose of the arrangements in question will be scrutinised to determine whether they create an activity, or an appearance of one, with the result that relief would be available (but for the "disqualifying" provision).

> "Examples might include (without necessarily being limited to):
>
> - cases where a business appears to be fragmented in a way which is commercially unusual with the result that there is a company which (apart from this test) meets the qualifying conditions for the schemes;
> - cases where a transaction which would normally be expected to be between two parties, involves three (or more) parties, where the additional party is a company which (apart from this test) meets the qualifying conditions for the schemes;
> - cases where the economic substance of a company's activity appears to be at odds with its form (for instance, where contractual arrangements appear designed to generate an outcome similar to a lending or credit facility whilst the contracts are not immediately obviously loan or credit contracts in legal form)."

Overall the provision is intended to prevent promoters offering EIS type products as an off the shelf solution for those seeking to avoid or mitigate tax with no real interest in entrepreneurial investment.

Where disqualifying arrangements are suspected by HMRC, the Small Companies Enterprise Centre (SCEC) may not be willing to issue an advance assurance opinion, meaning that the likelihood of a successful application for a compliance statement is less certain.

The only option if this is the case is to go ahead with the share issue, and apply via form EIS1. This can present a problem because the investors will often refuse to invest in the absence of an advance assurance opinion, as it gives the impression that HMRC view the company negatively in respect of EIS relief.

Of course it is worth remembering that an advance assurance opinion is not a guarantee of a subsequent application leading to a compliance statement being issued; though this is unlikely to appease investors who place reliance upon the assurance.

It might be possible to avoid employing any of the funds until after the application for the compliance statement has been made, and answer received. In the event of the application being unsuccessful the company could then always offer to repurchase the shares from the investors; however it could not be compelled to do so, or it would risk falling foul of the pre-arranged exits provisions discussed earlier (see **4.2.9**).

In any event, the use of such an arrangement would appear to be contrary to the intentions of EIS generally.

Law: ITA 2007, s. 178A
Guidance: VCM 12100

4.2.12 Risk to capital requirement

Finance Act 2018 contains a new condition for investments to ensure that they are made at full risk to the investor's capital. The new provision is included as s. 157A.

Over the years, a number of schemes have been marketed that purport to take advantage of EIS relief, but that are aimed at "capital preservation". This could be achieved by investment in a company, or portfolio of companies, where there is little chance of capital movement, either up or down. The idea is that after the termination date, the company buys back the shares at subscription price, and the investor has banked the 30% income tax relief.

From the point of view of the company, it is arguable that the investment constitutes an interest-free loan; however, in practice companies affiliated with a capital preservation scheme are likely to have been set up specifically to receive the investment and just about meet the requirements for relief to be given, undertaking a low-risk trade.

This is especially powerful if combined with inheritance tax planning, as EIS shares will generally qualify for business property relief after two years, and so there is a clear incentive for sheltering what would otherwise be taxable cash in this way, as the shares could be sold by the beneficiaries of the will.

Unsurprisingly, HMRC do not view these arrangements as genuine investments in the spirit of the EIS framework. Whilst the "no tax avoidance" requirement might catch them out, the new conditions are more explicit.

For investments made on or after 15 March 2018 (the date specified in the original tax policy note), relief will only be given if, at the time of the investment, it is reasonable to conclude that both:

- the investee company has an objective to grow and develop its trade in the long term; and
- there is a significant risk that the investor could lose more of the capital invested than he gets back by way of other returns from the investment.

The second condition means that investments that have little or no probability of anything but small movements in value – say plus or minus 10% – might not qualify, as this is far lower than the 30% income tax relief.

The condition will be assessed giving due consideration and regard to any circumstances existing at the time of the investment. The new s. 157A(3) sets out a non-exhaustive list of circumstances that will be considered:

(a) the extent to which the company's objectives include increasing the number of its employees or the turnover of its trade;

(b) the nature of the company's sources of income, including the extent to which there is a significant risk of the company not receiving some or all of the income;

(c) the extent to which the company has or is likely to have assets, or is or could become a party to arrangements for acquiring assets, that could be used to secure financing from any person;

(d) the extent to which the activities of the company are subcontracted to persons who are not connected with it;

(e) the nature of the company's ownership structure or management structure, including the extent to which others participate in or devise the structure;

(f) how any opportunity for investment in the company is marketed; and

(g) the extent to which arrangements are in place under which opportunities for investments in the company are or may be marketed with, or otherwise associated with, opportunities for investments in other companies or entities.

Law: ITA 2007, s. 157A

5. Income tax relief: withdrawal of relief

5.1 Overview

The preceding chapters mainly considered conditions which would preclude EIS relief from being granted on application. We will now consider situations where relief is initially granted, but has to be withdrawn due to a disqualifying event before the termination date.

In some cases, relief is only partially withdrawn, and a calculation is necessary to determine how much. This will consequently affect any loss relief claimed on the shares (if applicable), as the allowable loss is adjusted for any income tax relief given which has not yet been withdrawn. We will consider this in further detail later on.

It should be noted at the outset that HMRC have the power to raise a discovery assessment under TMA 1970, s. 29 if they discover that any of the information on the EIS1 form was incorrect. This can also attract a penalty if the information was submitted fraudulently or negligently.

Law: TMA 1970, s. 29

5.2 Changes of circumstances before termination date

As alluded to in the preceding chapters, a number of the specific conditions have to be met right up to the termination date of the relevant shares, not just at the date of the share issue. These conditions have been discussed in detail already; however those which need to be met throughout the holding period for the shares are summarised in the following table for ease of reference:

Condition	Relevant period	Chapter reference	Legislative reference (ITA 2007)
Investor must not become connected	A	2.3.2-2.3.6	s. 163
Company must be a trading company	B	3.2.4	s. 181-182

Condition	Relevant period	Chapter reference	Legislative reference (ITA 2007)
Company must carry out a qualifying activity	B	3.2.5	s. 183
Company can only control qualifying 51% subsidiaries, and must be independent	B	3.2.7	s. 185
All subsidiaries must be qualifying subsidiaries	B	3.2.10	s. 187
Any property management subsidiaries must be 90% subsidiaries	B	3.2.11	s. 188
Maximum risk finance investments company has raised cannot exceed £12 million (£20 million for knowledge-intensive companies)	B	4.2.4	s. 173AB

In addition to the above conditions, recall that the money raised by the share issue needs to be employed for a qualifying purpose within two years of the share issue date, or relief will be withdrawn – as was the case in *Skye Inns* and in *Benson Partnership*.

Cases: *Skye Inns Ltd and Mr Chris Richards v HMRC* [2009] UKFTT 366 (TC); *Benson Partnership Ltd v HMRC* [2012] UKFTT 63 (TC)

5.3 Disposal before termination date

5.3.1 Introduction

In addition to breaching the conditions set out in the table above, relief will be wholly or partly withdrawn in most circumstances where the investor makes a disposal of the shares before the termination date. Recall that the termination date is three years from the date of the share issue, or three years from the date that the qualifying trade commenced if this is later. The legislation actually refers to Period A; however, as it is impossible for the shares to be disposed before they are actually issued, we are only concerned in practice with the period beginning with the share issue date and ending with the termination date.

For this reason, it is essential to determine exactly when the share issue date is. This was discussed in **2.2.3**.

Relief is not withdrawn if the shares are transferred to a spouse or civil partner who is living with the investor at the time of the transfer.

Law: ITA 2007, s. 209

5.3.2 Disposal not at arm's length

If a disposal takes place before the end of Period A, and does not take place on arm's-length terms, the EIS relief will be withdrawn in full. This will automatically mean that any deferred gains will come back into charge immediately, and no automatic entitlement to share loss relief is enjoyed.

A bargain is generally held to be made at arm's-length if all parties to the transaction have acted in such a way as to get the best deal for themselves. The fact that an individual may not have got the best terms possible does not necessarily mean that the bargain was not made on arm's-length terms – the crucial factor is the intention. A bargain cannot be said to be made on arm's-length terms if there is an intention by one party to confer a gratuitous benefit on another. This would include a situation where a shareholder knowingly sells his shares for much less than they are worth.

Note that (contrary to popular misconception), a disposal may be held to have taken place otherwise than on arm's-length terms even if the parties are unconnected.

Law: ITA 2007, s. 209

5.3.3 Disposal at arm's length

Where an early disposal does take place on arm's-length terms, relief is only fully withdrawn if the sales proceeds are equal to or greater than the subscription price. Where the sales proceeds (if any) do not exceed the subscription price, a partial withdrawal of relief takes place. The amount of relief withdrawn is calculated using the following formula:

Relief withdrawn = sales proceeds x original rate of relief

Note that the relief is not simply withdrawn at 30%, because share issues made on or before 5 April 2011 would have attracted relief at 20%.

Example – withdrawal of relief

Meredith subscribed for 1,000 shares in EIS Ltd for £100,000 on 31 December 2014, claiming EIS income tax relief of £20,000. EIS Ltd did not start trading until 1 December 2016, meaning that the termination date for the shares is 1 December 2019. Meredith sold all her shares for £40,000 on 1 June 2018. This is before the termination date, despite being after the third anniversary of the investment.

The relief withdrawn will be 20% x £40,000 = £8,000. The remaining £12,000 is not withdrawn.

Where a partial withdrawal is made, the calculation for an allowable loss is affected as this depends on relief which was given but not withdrawn. This is discussed in **Chapter 6** below (loss relief).

The partial withdrawal provisions protect investors who have made genuine commercial investments, but who can clearly see that the company has not been successful. They can therefore cut their losses and receive at least some proceeds for the shares without being penalised by a full withdrawal of the relief.

Law: ITA 2007, s. 209

5.3.4 Part disposals

EIS relief given in respect of a particular share issue is treated as accruing evenly across all shares acquired. If, therefore, only part of the holding is sold prior to the termination date, only a proportion of the relief is withdrawn accordingly.

If the shares are sold for a marginal profit, the apportionment is fairly straightforward. So if 40% of the shares held are disposed before the termination date, 40% of the original relief will be withdrawn. The situation is slightly more complicated where the shares are sold at a loss.

Example – Meredith (continued) – part disposal

Consider Meredith's situation from above again; however, this time she only disposes of 600 shares for £25,000. Because the relief is deemed to accrue evenly over the subscription, these 600 shares account for £12,000 of the original relief.

The amount to be withdrawn will be £25,000 x 20% = £5,000. The remaining 400 shares account for £8,000 of EIS relief, and any further withdrawal cannot exceed this £8,000 – even if the shares are sold before the termination date at a profit. The relief not withdrawn on disposal of the 600 shares (i.e. £7,000) is never withdrawn.

One further consideration needed is the situation where full relief could not be utilised, for example where there was not sufficient income tax liability to use the maximum relief. In the circumstances, the calculation for the reduction is amended as follows:

> Relief withdrawn = sales proceeds x original rate of relief x A/B

where:

> A = the actual tax reduction given in £s
>
> B = the maximum possible tax reduction (i.e. qualifying investment x EIS rate).

Law: ITA 2007, s. 209-210

5.3.5 Liquidations

Where the reason for the disposal before the termination date is a liquidation entered into for genuine commercial reasons, the treatment depends on whether the liquidator makes any distribution to the shareholder before the termination date. If there is no such distribution then the proceeds used for calculating the withdrawal are £nil – and so no withdrawal is made.

If, however, some distribution is made by the liquidator, the amount will be treated as value received, and at least partial withdrawal will be necessary. The calculation of the withdrawal in these circumstances is considered later in this chapter.

Law: ITA 2007, s. 182

5.3.6 Reorganisations of share capital

In most circumstances, the takeover of the issuing company by another company will lead to EIS relief being withdrawn because of the requirement for it to be independent throughout Period B. If all the shares are sold for cash then all of the relief will be withdrawn, even if the sale is technically for a loss. This is because ceasing to meet the independence requirement would mean that the company is no longer a qualifying company.

In contrast, if a reorganisation involves the insertion of a brand new parent company above the issuing company, and the investors receive shares in the parent company in exchange for their own, relief may not necessarily be withdrawn. The circumstances where this applies are set out in s. 247. Broadly, clearance must have been given that HMRC are satisfied that the exchange has been made for genuine commercial reasons before this section can apply. The consideration for the old shares must consist solely of shares in the new parent company, and the acquiring company must acquire all of the shares in the issuing company.

One particular requirement is that the acquiring company is only permitted to have subscriber shares in issue. This means that following incorporation, no further shares are permitted to have been issued. To illustrate, consider a parent company founded by four shareholders holding a single share each. Section 247 can apply if this company, unchanged, takes over an issuing company by means of the qualifying share for share exchange. Conversely, if following the original founding of the company, some further shares are issued then s. 247 cannot apply. This (and the meaning of subscriber shares) was confirmed in the case of *Finn* where a reverse takeover method was adopted.

Law: ITA 2007, s. 247

Case: *Finn and Others v HMRC* [2015] UKFTT 144 (TC)

5.4 Options

If the relevant shares become subject to either a put or call option during the relevant period, this will also be treated as a disposal and all relief will be withdrawn.

A call option is one which would bind the investor to sell the shares to the option holder, or other nominated person. In practice, this could only occur after the investor acquires the shares, and so the relevant period under scrutiny is Period B.

A put option is one which would bind the grantor of the option to purchase the shares. In theory, this could take place prior to the shares being issued, and so the period under scrutiny is Period A.

Law: ITA 2007, s. 211-212

5.5 Value received

5.5.1 Introduction

EIS relief will be wholly or partially withdrawn if the investor receives value from the issuing company at any time during Period C. Recall that this begins 12 months prior to the share issue, and ends immediately before the termination date (see **2.2.1**).

The rule is extended to receipts that come from persons connected to the issuing company as well as just the company itself, and to situations where the recipient of the value is an associate of the investor.

Law: ITA 2007, s. 213

5.5.2 When is value received?

The occasions when value is considered as received for these purposes are set out by s. 216. Broadly, any payment made in respect of the relevant shares invested in – i.e. related to those shares – will be caught, other than certain exceptions which are set out accordingly in the section.

Example – value received

John invests in A Ltd during 2018. Shortly after the investment, the company repays a debt of £40,000 in respect of genuine services provided to the company by John. The credit is three months old, which is considered normal compared to other customers John has. This payment is not value received because it is discharged as an ordinary trade debt as per s. 216(2)(h).

Section 217 then sets out how to measure the amount of value received in each circumstance. HMRC guidance at VCM 15060 contains a handy table (reproduced below) combining the instances where value is received, with the measurement of that value. The table is useful, but is no substitute for familiarity with the contents of s. 216.

HMRC table reproduced from VCM 15060		
1	The company repays, redeems or repurchases any of its share capital or securities belonging to the individual.	The amount receivable or, if greater, the market value of the shares or securities.
2	The company makes a payment to the individual for giving up his right to any of its the shares or securities on their cancellation or extinguishment.	The amount receivable or, if greater, the market value of shares or securities market.
3	The company repays any debt owed to the individual. A debt incurred after the issue of the relevant shares is not taken into account for this, unless that debt replaced an earlier debt incurred before the share issue.	The amount receivable or, if greater, the value of the debt.
4	The company makes a payment to the individual for giving up his right to any debt on its extinguishment. ('ordinary trade debts' – see below – and debts in respect of payments listed at the VCM11060 are excepted from this rule).	The amount receivable or, if greater, the market value of the debt.
5	The company releases or waives any liability of the individual to the company. In addition to an actual release or waiver, a company is treated as having released or waived liability if the individual fails to discharge a liability owed to the company within 12 months of the time when it ought have been discharged.	The amount of the liability.
6	The company discharges, or undertakes to discharge, an individual's liability to a third person.	The amount of the liability.

HMRC table reproduced from VCM 15060		
7	The company makes a loan or advance to the individual other than one repaid in full before the issue of the shares.	The amount of the loan or advance.
8	The company provides a benefit or facility for the individual.	The cost to the company of providing the benefit facility less a consideration given for it by the individual.
9	The company transfers an asset to the individual for no consideration or consideration less than its market value.	The difference between the market value of the asset and any consideration given for it.
10	The individual transfers an asset to the company for a consideration in excess of its market value.	The difference between the market value of the asset and the consideration received for it.
11	The company makes any other payment to the individual, except payment within VCM11060 or one made in discharge of an 'ordinary trade debt' (see below).	The amount of the payment.
12	The individual receives any payment or asset in connection with the winding up or dissolution of the company.	The amount of the payment or market value of the asset.
13	The individual disposes of any share capital or securities, or rights over such shares etc., to a person connected with the company. See VCM15070	The amount receivable or, if greater, the market value of the shares.

Law: ITA 2007, s. 216, 217

Guidance: VCM 15060

5.5.3 Insignificant receipts

Value received will be ignored if it is insignificant. Insignificant means either:

- less than £1,000; or
- if more than £1,000, insignificant compared to the amount subscribed by the individual for the relevant shares.

If reliance is to be sought on the second point, then a subjective test will need to be carried out and agreement reached with HMRC.

Law: ITA 2007, s. 214

5.5.4 Withdrawal amount

The calculation to determine how much EIS relief must be withdrawn is virtually identical to that for a premature disposal (see **5.3** above). In the case of value received, however, the amount of the value replaces the sales proceeds in the formula. The provision for circumstances where EIS relief was not able to be claimed in full due to insufficient income is also the same.

Law: ITA 2007, s. 213, 220

5.5.5 Replacement value

Where value has been received, there is scope under s. 222 for the investor to return the value to the person that it was received from. This is referred to as replacement value. If the value was received by an associate, it is the associate who must return the value rather than the individual. Similarly, if the payment was made not by the issuing company but by a connected person, the return of value must go to that person.

In order for the provision to apply, the amount received must be returned in full – there is no credit given for a part return. It is possible that payments made to the appropriate person by the investor prior to the receipt of value can subsequently be classed as replacement value, provided it wasn't received before the start of Period C. The value must be replaced without unreasonable delay. In practice this means as soon as is reasonably possible following the discovery of the value receipt.

If the value received has been the subject of an appeals process, it needs to be replaced within 60 days of the final determination.

Law: ITA 2007, s. 222

5.6 Repayments of share capital

EIS relief enjoyed by the investor may be withdrawn if, during Period C, the company redeems or repurchases shares from any other shareholder, and that repurchase does not lead to a withdrawal of EIS, SEIS or CVS relief. Again the relief can be partial depending on the amount paid to the other shareholder(s).

The corporate venturing scheme (CVS) is not covered in this book, as it is no longer available for company investments after 31 March 2010; however due to the inclusion of the reference to it for the purposes of this provision, advisers may wish to avail themselves of the guidance beginning at VCM 90000.

The rule also applies if a subsidiary company is the one who repurchases the shares, even if it did not become a subsidiary until after the transaction had taken place.

The total amount of withdrawal of tax relief (for all EIS shareholders) is calculated by multiplying the EIS relief rate by the amount of the capital repayment. This withdrawal then has to be divided between any EIS shareholders in an appropriate proportion relative to their individual shareholdings. As can be seen, therefore, if the total capital repayment exceeds the total amount subscribed via EIS (in respect of shares when the termination date has not yet passed), relief will be withdrawn in full.

Note that this provision applies throughout Period C, and so any share repurchases in the 12 months prior to any prospective EIS investment would need to be considered.

A repayment can be ignored as insignificant if the actual amount paid, as well as the market value of the shares in respect of which it is paid, is insignificant. There is no stated threshold in the legislation, and HMRC therefore interpret insignificant as meaning trifling or unimportant.

The insignificant let out cannot be relied upon if the receipt is subject to any arrangements that were in existence in the 12 months prior to the share issue date.

Law: ITA 2007, s. 224-231

Guidance: VCM 90000ff.

5.7 Acquisition of trade or share capital

There are two provisions which aim to restrict EIS relief to genuine outside investors. These provisions prevent the issuing company from acquiring a trade previously carried on by the owners of the issuing company, or the share capital of a company which carried on the trade which the investor controlled.

The provision is different from the general conditions discussed at **4.2.6** regarding the use of the money. EIS will not be given if the money raised is used to purchase a trade or a majority shareholding in another company; however, the two provisions discussed below are still relevant because it is perfectly possible for the issuing company to acquire a trade or share capital using other funds, having employed the EIS money for a qualifying purpose.

Section 232 acts to withdraw any relief given to an individual if a trade (or the majority of the assets used to carry out a trade) is acquired by the issuing company, and at any time during Period A, the individual (alone or together with another group of individuals):

- owned more than a half share in the trade (unincorporated businesses); or
- controlled the company that previously carried on the trade (where the trade is carried on by a company).

As is often the case, the interests of any associated persons are aggregated with those of the individual for these purposes.

If the individual is a paid director, the time period is extended to any time before the end of Period A – i.e. if the director had more than a half share in a trade, or controlled the trading company at any time before the termination date of the shares, no relief can be given.

Note that the trade does not have to be acquired directly from the individual for the relief to be withdrawn.

Example – trade acquisition

Ben is a sole trader until he sells the trade to his friend Bill on 5 April 2018. On 31 December 2018 Ben invests in EIS Ltd claiming relief under EIS. Two years later EIS Ltd acquires the trade from Bill for genuine reasons. Because Ben owned the trade previously, the EIS relief has to be withdrawn.

Section 233 is essentially an identical provision, covering the situation where the shares of a company that carried on the trade are purchased by the issuing company instead of the trade and assets. The provision extending the relevant time period for paid directors is the same.

Law: ITA 2007, s. 232, 233

5.8 Relief found not to have been due

It is the responsibility of the investor or issuing company to notify HMRC in circumstances where their respective qualifying conditions are not met throughout the relevant time period. For example, the investor must notify HMRC if the relief needs to be withdrawn because he is no longer a qualifying investor, and the company must notify HMRC if it breaches the maximum permitted amount raised under risk finance investments during Period B.

HMRC have wide ranging powers to request information from investors, the issuing company, persons connected with it, or parties to any arrangements related to the share issue.

Section 234 gives HMRC the power to withdraw relief where the company does not give notice, and, in an officer's opinion:

- the company is not a qualifying company; or
- the shares were not issued to raise money for the purpose of a qualifying business activity; or
- the company using the money raised does not satisfy the conditions applying to it; or
- the money raised was not employed for the purpose of a qualifying business activity within the time allowed.

The officer must give notice to the issuing company (not the investor), stating the reason he intends to withdraw the relief. The company has the right to appeal the decision; however, the officer is entitled to raise assessments on the individual investors before the appeal is heard. This may be done to protect any assessment from falling out of time, though normally collection will not be sought before the appeal is heard – unless the arrangements are such that an accelerated payment notice may be issued.

Law: ITA 2007, s. 234

6. CGT: disposal and loss relief

6.1 CGT exemption

6.1.1 Overview

Where the shares issued under EIS are held throughout Period A before being disposed of, there are provisions in TCGA 1992 which can exempt any gain arising from CGT, whilst allowing any losses (subject to adjustment). Ordinarily, a disposal which would be exempt if it produced a gain cannot be allowable if it in fact produces a loss. An example of this would be qualifying corporate bonds (QCBs).

Gains will only be exempt if income tax relief has been claimed and not wholly withdrawn. Special consideration needs to be given to circumstances where relief has been withdrawn in part – for example because of a part disposal before the termination date.

Law: TCGA 1992, s. 150A

6.1.2 Income tax relief to have been claimed

An essential requirement of the CGT exemption is that income tax relief must have been claimed on the relevant shares. It is not sufficient that relief would have been available, there has to be at least some relief claimed by the investor. There has to be some reduction attributable to the EIS investment.

This requirement was examined in *Ames,* where the taxpayer had invested in qualifying shares, but not made any claim to EIS income tax relief because his income did not exceed the personal allowance for the year in question. There was also no scope to carry back the relief. As it transpired the only way to have done so would have been for him to disclaim part of the personal allowance, and as he had not done this within the prerequisite time limits HMRC refused his claim, as they did not feel that he had a reasonable excuse (for the lateness).

A point raised was that it appeared extremely unfair comparing the position of a person with no taxable income making an identical investment to a person with £1 of taxable income. The former would pay full CGT, whereas the second would pay nothing.

Law: TCGA 1992, s. 150A

Case: *Ames v HMRC* [2015] UKFTT 337 (TC)

6.1.3 Relief not withdrawn

Where income tax has been claimed and has not subsequently been withdrawn at all, a disposal after the end of Period A will be fully exempt in respect of the shares which attracted the EIS income tax relief. In the situation where the original investment was greater than the permitted annual limit, the exemption is available on a pro rata basis (discussed below).

Example – full exemption

Gemma invests £100,000 in EIS shares on 6 April 2015. The termination date relating to the shares is 6 April 2018. Gemma claims income tax relief and holds the shares for the required period. She sells the shares on 1 December 2018 for £400,000. The gain is exempt from CGT.

The disposal on which the exemption is being claimed should be included in the CGT summary pages on the tax return, with the relief then claimed to offset it, and an explanatory note inserted in the white space (i.e. the additional information box on the CGT summary pages).

Law: TCGA 1992, s. 150A

6.1.4 Relief partly withdrawn

If, during Period A, events transpire so that the original relief given is withdrawn in full, then any gain will be fully chargeable. The consideration will only be relevant if the shares continue to be held, so the only circumstances relevant when considering the partial availability of CGT relief are:

- where relief has been withdrawn due to receipt of value; or
- where relief has been withdrawn due to redemption or repayment of share capital made to other shareholders (see **5.5**).

It is (hopefully) fairly obvious that CGT exemption cannot be granted on shares which were disposed of before the termination date!

There is no restriction on the CGT exemption if EIS relief is not enjoyed in full solely because the individual did not have sufficient income tax liability to utilise the maximum relief available.

Example – partial income tax relief

Nicola subscribes for 300,000 shares at £1 each under EIS. Ordinarily the maximum relief would be £300,000 x 30% = £90,000; however her income tax liability for the year of investment and for the preceding year were £20,000 and £30,000 respectively. Utilising the carryback provision, her EIS relief enjoyed was therefore £50,000. This partial enjoyment does not restrict Nicola's claim to the CGT exemption in itself.

If, however, during period A there is a receipt of value, or redemption/repayment of share capital leading to a reduction in relief, there will be a restriction on the CGT exemption.

The restriction will depend on the reduction in income tax relief that arose from the receipt of value, or redemption/repayment accordingly. To calculate the amount of the gain that is no longer exempt, the following formula is used:

$$\text{Gain x } \frac{\text{The amount of reduction in income tax relief}}{\text{Total relief attributable to the shares}}$$

This is then deducted from the amount of the gain to find the remaining exempt part.

Example – value received

Suppose Nicola receives value of £50,000 during Period A. The reduction in EIS income tax relief is £15,000. Now assume that she sells the shares after the termination date for £500,000 – i.e. a gain of £200,000. Of this the exempt amount is:

$$£200{,}000 - \frac{£200{,}000 \times £15{,}000}{£50{,}000} = £140{,}000$$

The remaining £60,000 is a chargeable gain.

A further complication occurs where there is both a reduction due to receipt of value or redemption/repayment of capital, and an investment in excess of the permitted annual maximum. This is discussed at **6.1.5** below.

Law: TCGA 1992, s. 150B

6.1.5 Other restrictions

Relief will be restricted in circumstances where the original investment exceeded the maximum permitted amount for a year. The current maximum annual investment amount is £1 million, so if an investor bought shares for £2 million, disposal relief would be restricted to half of any gain arising on a disposal – or half of the total gains on a series of disposals. This maximum permitted amount is increased to £2 million insofar as the excess over the standard £1 million relates to investments in knowledge-intensive companies for investments made on or after a date to be appointed under FA 2018, Sch. 4, para. 1.

On each disposal, the gain arising is multiplied by the fraction given below to find the exemption:

$$\frac{\text{Income tax relief obtained}}{\text{EIS rate x total amount invested}}$$

So in the case of the investor discussed above, a sale for £5 million would give a total maximum exempt amount of:

$$\text{£3 million x } \frac{\text{£300,000}}{\text{30\% x £2 million}} = \text{£1.5 million}$$

The remaining £1.5 million of gain remains chargeable.

Trading losses

It is also important to recall that relief for trading losses which are offset against general income is given in priority to EIS relief – which is actually an income tax reducer.

If circumstances are such that a qualifying EIS investment is made and relief claimed, but a trading loss is later made which can be (and is) carried back to the year of the EIS investment to offset general income, the CGT exemption can be lost if the trading loss reduces the income tax liability to £nil – because the loss is relieved in priority to the EIS relief.

This could happen, for example, in circumstances where early years trading loss relief is available. Note that if there is some income tax liability left after the application of the loss, relief is not restricted.

Excess investment and reduction of relief

As discussed above briefly, a complicated situation arises where there is both an excessive initial investment (i.e. one which is in excess of the permitted annual maximum) and the reduction in income tax relief during Period A because of, for example, a receipt of value.

To determine correctly how much of any subsequent gain is exempt, the first step is to calculate the exempt gain following an excessive investment (so £1.5 million in the case of the investor discussed above). This now becomes the maximum exempt gain. This figure then replaces the total gain figure used to determine the deduction in the formula given in **6.1.4** (i.e. calculating the restriction following a partial withdrawal of relief).

Representing this in formulaic form in full, this gives us:

$$\text{Gain (reduced)} - \left[\text{Gain (reduced)} \times \frac{\text{Amount of reduction in income tax relief}}{\text{Total relief attributable to the shares}}\right]$$

where Gain (reduced) is:

$$\text{Total gain} \times \frac{\text{Income tax relief obtained}}{\text{EIS rate x total amount invested}}$$

A worked example is given at VCM 20090, reproduced below:

HMRC example

In this example TCGA92/S150A(3) applies to restrict the exemption.

- July 2008 investor subscribes £750,000 for 100,000 shares in an EIS company. Maximum Income Tax relief of £100,000 is given in the tax year 2008-9.
- August 2009 the investor receives £100,000 value from the company. The Income Tax relief is reduced by £13,333 (£20,000 x £100,000 / £150,000) by making an assessment.
- January 2013 all the shares are sold for £1,350,000.

The chargeable gain is calculated as below:

Disposal proceeds	£1,350,000
Less cost	£750,000
Chargeable gain	£600,000

The TCGA92/S150A (3) formula is:

$$\frac{A}{B} = \frac{\text{Amount of tax relief}}{\text{Subscription x EIS rate (20\% 2008 - 09)}} = \frac{£100{,}000}{£150{,}000}$$

The chargeable gain exemption is restricted to £600,000 x 2/3 = £400,000 leaving a chargeable gain at this point of £200,000.

The exemption is further reduced by the following amount:

$$\text{Exempt gain x } \frac{\text{Reduction in relief}}{\text{Relief atributable to shares before the reduction}}$$

$$£400{,}000 \text{ x } \frac{£13{,}333}{£100{,}000} = £53{,}333$$

The exempt gain becomes £346,667 and the chargeable gain £253,333 (£200,000 + £53,333).

Law: TCGA 1992, s. 150A(3), 150B

Guidance: VCM 13030

6.1.6 *Entrepreneurs' relief*

If there is a restriction on the amount of gain which is eligible for the CGT exemption then the question should be considered of whether entrepreneurs' relief is available on the remainder. Whilst an in-depth look at entrepreneurs' relief is beyond the scope of this publication, relief will generally be available on the EIS type companies provided the personal company test is met:

- the shareholder must have held at least 5% of the ordinary share capital for at least 12 months prior to disposal; and
- the shareholder must have been an employee or officer of the company for at least 12 months prior to disposal.

The reference to ordinary share capital means that the investor must have held at least 5% of the nominal value of the total issued share capital, and the attached rights thereon (i.e. voting rights and rights to capital upon a winding up).

Law: TCGA 1992, s. 169H

6.1.7 Revived gains

It should not be overlooked that the disposal of EIS shares may result in deferred gains coming back into charge where CGT deferral relief was claimed at the time of the investment (or later as applicable).

Deferral relief will be looked at in the next chapter; however, one important point is a furtherance to the previous section on entrepreneurs' relief: since 3 December 2014, any gains which are deferred using EIS deferral relief, which would have qualified for entrepreneurs' relief in the absence of the deferral claim, will similarly be eligible for entrepreneurs' relief upon revival when the EIS shares are sold.

Law: TCGA 1992, s. 169T

6.2 Losses

6.2.1 Generally

As mentioned in the overview, in most circumstances where a disposal would be exempt from CGT if it produced a gain, any loss arising on such a disposal would be non-allowable. This works because the legislation specifically disapplies the provision preventing a disposal from being a chargeable event where a loss arises.

In calculating the loss, the allowable costs have to be reduced by the amount of income tax relief given and not subsequently withdrawn.

Example: restriction of capital loss

Penelope invests £1 million in shares in an EIS qualifying company, claiming the full £300,000 EIS income tax relief. No relief is withdrawn. The shares eventually become worthless and the company is liquidated. The capital loss of £1 million is reduced by the £300,000 income tax relief given and not withdrawn, meaning the allowable loss is £700,000.

In the event that there is only a part disposal, the reduction is made on a pro rata basis.

Example: restriction for part disposal

Thomas invests £1 million in shares in an EIS qualifying company, claiming the full £300,000 EIS income tax relief, which is not subsequently withdrawn. He later sells half of the shares for £50,000. The loss of £450,000 is reduced by £150,000 (i.e. half of the income tax relief not withdrawn).

Law: TCGA 1992, s. 150A

6.2.2 Offsetting losses against general income

Losses arising on disposals of "qualifying shares" may be offset against general income rather than against other capital gains.

Shares are automatically qualifying shares for these purposes if EIS relief is attributable to them. Because of the wording of the legislation, it would not matter if (following the end of the minimum holding period) the company had ceased to carry on a qualifying trade.

Where losses are to be relieved against general income, they can be relieved against income for the year the loss arose in, the preceding year, or both. It may be necessary to offset both the years' income if the loss exceeds the income for one of the years. If a claim is being made to relieve income in both tax years, the taxpayer should specify on his return which year is to be offset first.

There is a general restriction on sideways loss relief introduced by FA 2013. This restriction limits the maximum offset of the capital loss against income to the higher of:

- £50,000; or
- 25% of the taxpayer's income.

Losses arising on EIS shares which are to be relieved against income *do not* fall within the provisions of this cap – found in ITA 2007, s. 24A – because restrictions are already imposed upon maximum investment amounts attracting relief. This is confirmed by

s. 24A (7). Losses in excess of the general restriction limit can therefore be relieved in full provided that they are shares to which EIS relief is attributable.

Having identified that share loss relief is available due to attributable EIS relief, and that there is income to offset, normal procedures for claiming share loss relief should be followed (found in ITA 2007, s. 133).

If all of the loss cannot be relieved against income in the relevant two years (because there is not enough income to relieve the loss fully), the unused balance can be used against capital gains arising in the same year as the loss, or carried forward to offset future capital gains.

Law: ITA 2007, s. 24A, 131, 133

6.3 Reorganisations

6.3.1 Bonus issues

A bonus issue is an event where existing shareholders are given additional shares, usually calculated by reference to their existing holding (e.g. one new share for every two existing shares). Provided that the bonus issue is made in this way, the bonus shares will be treated as if they were acquired at the same time as the existing shares. The income tax relief attributable to each share is simply spread across more shares, and so the shares can qualify for the disposal relief in the event of a part disposal.

Law: TCGA 1992, s. 150A(6)

6.3.2 Rights issues

In contrast, a rights issue is an opportunity (i.e. right) to participate in a further share issue in exchange for a subscription. The new shares are treated for the purposes of EIS relief as a separate investment to the original shares, and so the qualifying conditions will need to be met at the time of the rights issue if EIS income tax relief (and therefore disposal relief) is to apply.

Law: TCGA 1992, s. 150A(7)

6.3.3 *Share exchanges*

When another company wants to acquire the EIS company, it may do so by purchasing all of the shares. This could lead to a withdrawal of income tax relief for the individual shareholders if it occurs before the termination date of the shares. A purchase in this way will also be a disposal for CGT purposes, and so the conditions necessary for disposal relief will need to be considered.

Alternatively, the acquiring company could take over the EIS company by issuing its own shares in exchange for the existing share capital. The EIS shareholders subsequently become shareholders in the parent company. The consequences for any income tax relief are discussed at **5.3.6**.

Ordinarily on a takeover actioned by a share exchange, the new shares are treated as standing in the shoes of the old shares, and no disposal is deemed to have taken place for CGT purposes. For exchanges involving EIS shares, the general rule is that the exchange constitutes a disposal for CGT purposes (i.e. it is a chargeable event). Recall that if a disposal occurs before the termination date, disposal relief is not available.

This general rule (which disapplies TCGA 1992, s. 135-137) applies to any takeover of shares which were issued under EIS, unless:

- all income tax relief obtained on the shares has been withdrawn (this could result from the takeover itself, if the conditions in ITA 2007, s. 247 are not met); or
- not all the income tax relief is withdrawn, but:
    - the exchange takes place after the termination of the original share issue, and the conditions in (1) below are met, or
    - the conditions in (2) are met.

1. ***Takeover by another EIS company***

If:

- one EIS qualifying company, that is a company which has issued one or more compliance certificates (EIS3), takes over a second EIS qualifying company; and

- the new holding consists of new ordinary shares issued by the acquiring EIS company after the termination date referred to above that carry no present or future preferential rights to dividends or to assets on a winding up, and no present or future rights to be redeemed,

then the ordinary "no disposal" position set out in s. 135 will apply, provided that the anti-avoidance provisions in s. 137 (no tax avoidance motive etc.) are not applicable.

2. *Takeover by new parent company*

Where:

- a company, having issued only subscriber shares, acquires all the shares (and securities) in an EIS company in exchange only for the proportionate issue of its own shares (and securities) of a corresponding description, that is carrying the same essential rights as the old shares; and
- before the issue of the new shares (and securities), HMRC have notified the new company or the old company that they are satisfied that the share exchange will take place for bona fide commercial reasons and will not form part of any such scheme or arrangements as are mentioned in TCGA 1992, s. 137,

no disposal is deemed to take place, and the shares stand in the place of the original shares.

Law: TCGA 1992, s. 150A(8A-8D); Sch. 5B, para. 8, 9

7. CGT: deferral relief

7.1 Overview

An investor making a qualifying EIS investment is entitled to match up to the amount invested to any capital gains made within a specified time window (relative to the investment).

Additionally, an investor who does not qualify for EIS income tax relief may still be able to claim CGT deferral relief, as the rules regarding who can claim are less stringent. For example there is no requirement that the investor must not be connected to the company to claim deferral relief.

Matched gains are then deferred, and do not fall to be charged to CGT until the EIS shares are later disposed of, or until another chargeable event arises. It must be realised that it is the gain itself which is deferred, and not the tax. This is an important distinction because revived gains are charged at the prevailing rate of CGT in the year in which they are revived. Therefore if the CGT rates increase, more tax may eventually be payable than would have been if the deferral had not been claimed.

In many cases, the qualifying conditions for deferral relief in the legislation refer directly to the conditions and definitions for income tax relief we have discussed above. Where appropriate, reference will be made to the sections in the relevant chapter accordingly.

The majority of the relevant legislation applicable to deferral relief is contained within Schedule 5B of TCGA 1992.

Law: TCGA 1992, Sch. 5B

7.2 Qualifying investments

7.2.1 Qualifying time window

In order to be capable of being matched to an EIS investment, the gains must arise within a four-year time window, commencing three years before, and ending one year after the share issue date.

An alternative way of thinking about this is that once the taxpayer realises any capital gains, he has three years to make an EIS investment and defer some or all of them, or he can match them to an EIS investment made within the preceding 12 months.

In some circumstances, HMRC have the power to extend the qualifying time where the EIS investment was not made within three years. Guidance as to when HMRC will do this is contained within VCM 23030, which states that the time limit will be extended where the claimant can show that he or she:

- had a firm intention to comply with the time limit, but
- was prevented by some fact or circumstance beyond his or her control from complying, and
- acted as soon as he or she reasonably could after ceasing to be so prevented.

It is clear, therefore, that the onus to demonstrate this is on the taxpayer. The guidance also confirms that each case will be considered on its merits.

Law: TCGA 1992, Sch. 5B, para. 1(3)
Guidance: VCM 23030

7.2.2 Gains that can be deferred

Gains that arise from actual disposals of assets can be deferred, as can gains which crystallise because of the disposal of shares – for example gains deferred under an earlier EIS investment. Additionally, certain gains arising on deemed disposals – for example where a revived gain comes back into charge due to the EIS shares ceasing to be eligible shares – can also be deferred.

A gain cannot be deferred using EIS deferral relief if it arises from a disposal of shares in the same company as the one into which the EIS investment is being made.

Law: TCGA 1992, Sch. 5B, para. 1(3)

7.2.3 Eligible claimants

Only UK resident individuals and trustees of a qualifying UK resident settlement can claim deferral relief. A qualifying settlement is broadly one where all beneficiaries are either individuals or charities.

An individual cannot claim deferral relief if he or she is dual resident, and would be treated as resident in another country under the relevant double tax treaty. Additionally, no relief is available if the circumstances are such that if the EIS shares were sold immediately after purchase at a gain, they would not be chargeable to CGT.

There is no restriction on connected individuals claiming EIS deferral relief; therefore, existing paid directors, and those with a material interest (i.e. more than 30% of the ordinary share capital) are eligible to claim.

Law: TCGA 1992, Sch. 5B, para. 1

7.2.4 Maximum amount to be deferred

At the time of writing there is no current restriction on the amount of an individual's gains which can be deferred by qualifying investments. However, it is important to recall the gross assets test and the effect that a particularly large investment in a single company intended to attract deferral relief might have. This is because in order for an investment to be an eligible investment for the purposes of deferral relief, the issuing company has to meet the qualifying company status as set out in the provisions for the income tax relief.

Additionally, the maximum amount that can be raised annually by the issuing company (currently £5 million) may come into play. Even if the investor is not intending to claim income tax relief (perhaps because he or she is connected to the issuing company), any amount raised through an EIS issue on which deferral relief is to be claimed also counts as relevant investments for the purposes of the cap.

This is because in order to claim deferral relief a compliance certificate has to be obtained from HMRC, and relevant investments for the purposes of the annual maximum are defined as those to which a compliance certificate has been so obtained.

The legislation in its current form does not make reference to the new lifetime maximum introduced from 18 November 2015 for the purposes of CGT deferral relief.

If the investor is looking to make an investment which would mean the annual maximum relevant investments limit would be breached, he would need to invest in more than one qualifying company – possibly through an approved EIS fund.

7.2.5 Summary of qualifying conditions

As mentioned in the overview, many of the qualifying conditions for deferral relief are identical to corresponding conditions for the income tax relief. Rather than repeat these, the qualifying conditions for deferral relief have been summarised in the table below, and where applicable the reference to the paragraph containing the condition is given for the purposes of cross referral.

Condition	Reference
The investor must be UK resident at the time the gain to be deferred arises, and at the time the qualifying EIS investment is made.	n/a
The issuing company must be a qualifying company.	Chapter 3
The shares must be eligible shares issued within the qualifying time, and where the share issue date is before the accrual time (i.e. when the gain to be deferred arises), the issued shares must still be held by the investor.	4.2.2
The shares must be subscribed for wholly in cash and fully paid up at the time they are issued.	4.2.2
The shares must be subscribed, and issued, for bona fide commercial reasons and not as part of arrangements the main purpose or one of the main purposes of which is the avoidance of tax.	4.2.10
The shares must be issued to raise money for the purpose of a qualifying business activity.	4.2.5
The qualifying business activity must be carried out by the issuing company, or a qualifying 90% subsidiary thereof.	4.1

Condition	Reference
All of the money raised must be employed wholly for the purpose of the qualifying activity by the relevant deadline.	4.2.6

Law: TCGA 1992, Sch. 5B, para. 1, 19

7.3 Mechanics of relief

Deferral relief cannot be claimed before a compliance statement is issued by HMRC. This can mean in practice that the CGT has to be paid in the meantime and reclaimed later on.

Unlike business asset rollover relief, no adjustment is made to the base cost of the new shares to give effect to the deferral. Instead, the amount of gain being deferred is simply suspended until a chargeable event occurs.

There is no stipulation as to which gains have to be deferred – i.e. earlier gains do not have to be deferred first, it is entirely the taxpayer's choice. A relevant entry should be made on the CGT summary pages of the self-assessment tax return showing which gain the taxpayer has chosen to defer.

It will generally be preferable to defer a gain that would otherwise be taxable at 10% or 20%, rather than one to which the entrepreneurs' relief rate will apply, as this will provide the greatest upfront saving and won't eat into the lifetime allowance for entrepreneurs' relief. Note that the lower general rate of 10% only applies to the extent that the individual's income hasn't exhausted his or her basic rate band. It should, however, also be recalled that when a revived gain is eventually charged, it will be charged at the prevailing rate of CGT in the year of revival. This could mean that the gain that would have suffered CGT at 20% is eventually charged at a higher rate.

Additionally, it is worth noting that since 3 December 2014, a gain which would qualify for entrepreneurs' relief can be deferred via EIS without losing the entitlement. Whilst this is definitely a positive announcement, the differential with the top tax rate if the entrepreneurs' rate were scrapped at some point in the future (as many commentators speculate) would need to be considered.

The relief simply takes the form of a direct £1 for £1 offset. A record of which gains have been deferred, and the underlying details, should be kept to enable accurate future calculation.

Law: TCGA 1992, Sch. 5B, para. 2

7.4 Reviving gains: chargeable events

A deferred gain will be revived in whole or in part where a chargeable event occurs. The legislation sets out five instances of such a chargeable event:

- the investor disposes of the relevant shares, other than to a spouse or civil partner;
- a spouse or civil partner, having acquired the shares from the investor, disposes of the shares to a third party;
- the investor becomes non-UK resident whilst holding the shares, where the date the non-residency began precedes the termination date of the shares (see below);
- a spouse or civil partner who acquired the shares becomes non-UK resident prior to the termination date (see below); or
- the shares cease to be eligible shares, or are treated for the purposes of the deferral relief legislation as so ceasing.

In respect to the third and fourth conditions, as an exception to the general rule, that will not be a chargeable event if the reason for the non-residency is to take up a position of employment or office of which all the duties are performed outside the UK, and if UK residency recommences within three years. This is subject to the further condition that the shares were not sold during the non-resident period.

Additionally, it is confirmed that the death of the investor, or of a spouse or civil partner to whom the shares have been transferred, is not treated as a chargeable event. This means that if an investor dies following a successful EIS deferral relief claim, the gain deferred will effectively die with him.

Law: TCGA 1992, Sch. 5B, para. 3

7.5 Reviving gains: shares ceasing to be eligible

7.5.1 Introduction

The relevant shares will cease to be treated as eligible shares, therefore triggering the revival of a gain, in a number of circumstances. Many of these circumstances are similar to those contained within the provisions governing the withdrawal of income tax relief.

There are, however, some important differences, particularly with regard to relevant periods. For this reason, the deferral relief provisions do not directly refer to the income tax relief provisions, even though the main body of the provision may be identical to its counterpart.

Law: TCGA 1992, Sch. 5B, para. 19

7.5.2 Put and call options

The meaning of put and call options was discussed at **5.4**. The meaning is the same for the purposes of deferral relief. Where such options are granted on or before the share issue date, the shares in question will never be eligible shares.

Where the option date is after the date of the shares, but before the end of the relevant period, a disposal (and therefore a chargeable event) is treated as taking place on the date of the option grant.

The relevant period referred to is Period A, i.e. starting two years before the share issue date, and ending immediately before the termination date of the relevant shares.

Law: TCGA 1992, Sch. 5B, para. 3

7.5.3 Linked loans

If at any time in the relevant period a linked loan is made to the investor (or to any associate of his or hers), the shares will be treated either as not eligible (if the loan was made prior to the share issue date), or as ceasing to be eligible (if afterwards).

Again the relevant period is period A. See **2.3.7** for in-depth commentary on linked loans.

Law: TCGA 1992, Sch. 5B, para. 15

7.5.4 Disqualifying arrangements

No deferral relief can be claimed if the shares are issued in consequence, anticipation, or otherwise in connection with disqualifying arrangements. See **4.2.11** for the meaning of disqualifying arrangements.

Law: TCGA 1992, Sch. 5B, para. 11A

7.5.5 Pre-arranged exits

Shares will not be treated as eligible if there are arrangements related to their issue that constitute pre-arranged exits, as discussed at **4.2.9**.

Law: TCGA 1992, Sch. 5B, para. 11

7.5.6 Value received

The value received provisions which serve to withdraw income tax relief (see **5.4**) are equally applicable to deferral relief. The deferral period will therefore end if the investor receives value within the "period of restriction". The period of restriction is Period C, i.e. beginning one year before the share issue date and ending immediately before the termination date.

The definition of when value is received is similar, but not identical, to that contained within ITA 2007. For the avoidance of doubt, value is received according to Sch. 5B of TCGA 1992 in the following circumstances (reproduced):

> "13(2) For the purposes of this paragraph an individual receives value from the company if the company–
>
> (a) repays, redeems or repurchases any of its share capital or securities which belong to the individual or makes any payment to him for giving up his right to any of the company's share capital or any security on its cancellation or extinguishment;
>
> (b) repays, in pursuance of any arrangements for or in connection with the acquisition of the shares, any debt owed to the individual other than a debt which was incurred by the company–

(i) on or after the date of issue of the shares; and

(ii) otherwise than in consideration of the extinguishment of a debt incurred before that date;

(c) makes to the individual any payment for giving up his right to any debt on its extinguishment;

(d) releases or waives any liability of the individual to the company or discharges, or undertakes to discharge, any liability of his to a third person;

(e) makes a loan or advance to the individual which has not been repaid in full before the issue of the shares;

(f) provides a benefit or facility for the individual;

(g) disposes of an asset to the individual for no consideration or for a consideration which is or the value of which is less than the market value of the asset;

(h) acquires an asset from the individual for a consideration which is or the value of which is more than the market value of the asset; or

(i) makes any payment to the individual other than a qualifying payment."

Qualifying payments include reasonable remuneration for services, allowable expenses, payment for goods or assets which do not exceed a market value, or ordinary dividends not exceeding a normal rate of return.

The provisions regarding insignificant receipts of value being ignored, and the ability to make a return or repayment of value to avoid relief being withdrawn, are the same in practice under the deferral relief provisions as they are under the income tax relief provisions; the only difference is the way the legislation is worded. Therefore, refer to **5.4.3** for a full discussion.

Law: TCGA 1992, Sch. 5B, para. 13

7.5.7 Breach of qualifying conditions

As discussed above, there are a number of qualifying conditions to be met before deferral relief can be claimed. If one or more if these conditions is breached within Period A, a chargeable event occurs. The conditions are summarised below, along with the date the corresponding chargeable event is treated as occurring.

Event	Date of chargeable event
Company ceases to be a qualifying company	The date the company ceases to be so qualifying
Qualifying activity is not carried on by issuing company or qualifying 90% subsidiary	The date the activity ceased being carried out by the issuing company or qualifying 90% subsidiary
Money raised was not intended to be used for the purposes of a qualifying business activity	Shares will be treated as never eligible – deferment will be reversed and cancelled.
Money was intended to be used for the purposes of a qualifying activity, but was not employed before the deadline	The date the deadline passes, unless the claim not yet made in which case shares will never be treated as eligible shares.

Law: ITA 2007, Pt. 5, Ch. 3-4

7.6 Assessing the gain

7.6.1 Overview

Where one of the events above transpires, at least some of the deferral will end and the corresponding suspended gain will be revived. Where the reason for the deferral coming to an end is not a disposal, the deferral will be removed in full. In the event of a part disposal, the deferral relief will be withdrawn on a pro-rated basis, subject to special matching rules.

A notable difference between deferral relief and income tax relief is that the receipt of value which is not subsequently replaced will give rise to the removal of deferral relief in full. There is therefore no need to ascertain the amount of value received in determining how much relief is removed (although it still may be necessary if the intention is to replace the value).

Because the granting of a put or call option over shares within Period A is treated as a disposal, it may be possible that relief is only partially withdrawn if it can be shown that the option only affects some of the shares.

Law: TCGA 1992, Sch. 5B, para. 4

7.6.2 Mixed holdings

Where there is only a single subscription of shares to which deferral relief applies, it is relatively straightforward to identify the revived gain. For example if 100,000 shares were issued at £1 each, and were used in full to defer a gain of £100,000, a disposal of all the shares will bring £100,000 pounds of gain back into charge, a disposal of 30,000 shares will bring in £30,000 of gain and so on.

In some circumstances it may transpire that an investor holds a mix of shares in the issuing company acquired on the same day that attracted either income tax relief, CGT deferral relief, both, or neither depending on the particular prevailing conditions at the time the respective share issues took place. If this is the case then the shares disposed must be carefully identified in accordance with the special identification rules set out in TCGA 1992, Sch. 5B, para. 4.

The identification rules are relatively easy to follow, and essentially provide that the shares are not pooled as normally, but are treated as being disposed on a first-in first-out basis. In circumstances where shares attracting different relief are required on the same day, the rules stipulate that shares to which no relief is attached are treated as being disposed first, followed by shares only attracting deferral relief, shares only attracting income tax relief, and finally shares attracting both.

Law: TCGA 1992, Sch. 5B, para. 4

7.7 Reorganisations and reconstructions

When a buying firm purchases all the share capital in a target which has issued shares under EIS there is a disposal, and so any deferred gains will be revived. In practice, however, it is often the case that the buying company will issue its own shares in exchange for existing shares in the target company. Whether or not this causes a gain to be revived is complex. HMRC's guidance at VCM 23230 should be referred to.

There is a distinction between shares which initially attracted both income tax relief and deferral relief, and those where only deferral relief was claimed – for example where a connected individual made the investment.

Deferral relief only

The general rule is that the deferred gain will be revived, except for occasions where either of the following conditions are met (reproduced from VCM 23230):

"1. Where:

- on or after 6 April 1998 a company, having issued only subscriber shares, acquires all the shares (and securities) in an EIS qualifying company in exchange for the proportionate issue of its own shares (and securities) of a corresponding description, see VCM23240, and
- the anti-avoidance provisions of TCGA92/S137 do not apply, see CG52505

the share exchange is treated as not involving a disposal of the original shares, and the new shares stand in the place of the old shares in all respects and attract the same deferral relief, see example at VCM23250. ...

2. Where:

- one EIS qualifying company, that is a company which has issued one or more EIS3 certificates takes over a second EIS qualifying company, and
- the acquiring EIS qualifying company issues its own ordinary shares carrying no present or future preferential rights etc. in exchange for the original shares more than five years after the original shares were issued, or where the original shares were issued on or after 6 April 2000, on or after the termination date, see VCM23070, relating to the original shares,

TCGA92/S135 applies if its conditions are met and the anti-avoidance provisions of TCGA92/S137 do not operate, see

CG52500 onwards. This is not treated as a disposal and the deferred gain will not be brought back into charge on the share exchange and there is no crystallisation of any gain or loss on the shares."

Income tax relief and deferral relief

Where the shares originally attracted income tax relief as well a slightly different situation arises, because it is necessary to consider the position regarding disposal relief (i.e. the CGT exemption on the EIS shares themselves), which relies on there being a claim to income tax relief that has not been withdrawn.

Again the general rule is that a takeover will trigger both a disposal of the EIS shares and lead to a deferred gain being revived, unless one of the two situations described in VCM 23230 applies.

The first situation involves the takeover by a clean holding company. In HMRC's words, we are concerned with circumstances where:

- "on or after 6 April 1998 a company, having issued only subscriber shares, acquires all the shares (and securities) in an EIS qualifying company in exchange for the proportionate issue of its own shares (and securities) of a corresponding description, see VCM23240, and
- the anti-avoidance provisions of TCGA92/S137 do not apply, see CG52505."

In these circumstances, the exchange will not be treated as a disposal, and so the deferred gain will not come back into charge, and there is no crystallisation of any gain or loss on the EIS shares.

The second situation is the takeover by another EIS company. Again, it is helpful to use HMRC's wording, namely where

- "one EIS qualifying company, that is a company which has issued one or more EIS3 certificates takes over a second EIS qualifying company, and
- the acquiring EIS qualifying company issues its own ordinary shares carrying no present or future preferential rights etc. in exchange for the original shares more than five years after the original shares were issued, or where

> the original shares were issued on or after 6 April 2000, on or after the termination date, see VCM23070, relating to the original shares."

In this second scenario, the takeover is not treated as a disposal, the deferred gain will not be brought back into charge, and there is no crystallisation of any gain or loss on the EIS shares.

Law: TCGA 1992, Sch. 5B, para. 8
Guidance: VCM 23230

Venture Capital Trusts

8. Introduction

8.1 History

The Venture Capital Trust (VCT) was first mooted by the Conservative Chancellor Kenneth Clarke in his November 1993 Budget speech. The actual content contained in the speech itself was fairly limited:

> "I also intend to create a new type of investment, a Venture Capital Trust, which will channel savings specifically into unquoted trading companies. Investors will receive dividends and capital gains entirely free of tax. By investing through a trust, they will also be able to spread their risk across a number of different companies. My hon. Friend the Financial Secretary will shortly be issuing a consultation paper fleshing out the details."

The intention was clearly to make further incentives available to private investors looking to provide finance to small companies. The Enterprise Investment Scheme was already established at this point; however a key difference is contained within the speech itself – the ability to spread risk.

Following a period of consultation, the VCT was introduced by FA 1995. Initially, tax relief was restricted to £100,000 of shares per year, with the income tax reducer set at 20%. Until 2004, investors could also use VCT investments to defer capital gains tax in the same way as is allowed for EIS investments.

From the outset, VCTs were designed to be fundamentally less risky (relative to EIS investments) as the investor's money is spread across several companies. VCTs are required to use investments raised to fund smaller unquoted companies, and are heavily restricted in terms of what they can invest into; however VCTs are permitted to invest a proportion of their funds in publicly listed companies.

Because of this lower inherent risk, the tax incentives are not as generous as the EIS scheme.

Law: ITA 2007, Pt. 6

8.2 Nature

Despite their name, VCTs are actually companies. The word trust in the name is therefore slightly misleading; however, it remains relevant because the structure is similar to an investment trust. A VCT has to be formally approved by HMRC, and must be traded on a regulated stock exchange.

In practice, this means that – from the investor's point of view – there is far less red tape to go through when it comes to making an investment. Investors simply need to find the profile of a VCT which has already received approval and invest accordingly.

8.3 Scope of this section

In this section we will cover the tax reliefs available to the investor, and look broadly at the conditions that a VCT must meet to become approved. We will not cover the formal reporting requirements, or tax exemptions of the VCT itself in any great detail, as this book is intended to be a guide (in the main) for investors (and their professional advisers) rather than an operating guide to running a VCT.

8.4 Summary of tax reliefs

An approved VCT is exempt from corporation tax on any chargeable gains it makes. It cannot, however, use any losses of a capital nature to offset other income.

From the investor's point of view there are three aspects to the relief, considered below. Note that the ability to defer CGT on gains by using VCT investments was removed for investments made on or after 6 April 2004.

8.4.1 Front end income tax relief

An investor who makes a qualifying investment in a VCT is entitled to an income tax reduction of 30% on a maximum of £200,000 of shares per tax year.

Example

Millie invests £120,000 in 2018-19. She is entitled to claim an income tax reduction of £36,000.

The income tax reduction cannot reduce the overall tax liability for the year below £nil. If Millie's tax liability in the example above was only £20,000, she would be restricted to claiming a reduction of £20,000 accordingly.

Law: ITA 2007, s. 262, 263

8.4.2 Dividend tax exemption

Any dividends paid on qualifying investments up to the permitted maximum of £200,000 of shares per tax year will be exempt from income tax. If the permitted maximum investment amount is exceeded, then dividends on the first £200,000 will be exempt; however tax will be payable on dividends paid on the excess shares.

Law: ITTOIA 2005, s. 709-712

8.4.3 CGT exemption

Shares acquired within the permitted annual maximum will be exempt from CGT upon a subsequent disposal, subject to ongoing conditions discussed later. Again if there are shares in excess of the permitted maximum investment limit, then only the shares acquired within the limits will be exempt. The excess shares will be fully chargeable to CGT.

When looking at the permitted maximum annual investment, shares acquired earlier in the year will be treated for these purposes as being acquired first. For this reason it is important that good records are kept to ensure that any taxable dividends or gains can be correctly reported.

Law: TCGA 1992, s. 151A

9. The approved VCT

9.1 Overview

In order to be able to offer shares as a VCT, a company must apply in writing to the Small Companies Enterprise Centre (SCEC) for formal approval. There is no specific form to be completed.

In order to receive approval, the company must meet a number of conditions, one of which is that it must not be a close company.

Whilst the law and reporting requirements of a VCT are not covered in great detail in this publication, a general overview of the qualifying conditions that must be met is provided to a degree that is likely to be of interest to sophisticated investors.

Law: ITA 2007, s. 274

9.2 Full approval

Approval of a VCT can be full or provisional. If a potential VCT company has not yet met the requirements for full approval, provisional approval may be granted with a view to full approval (so allowing qualifying VCT investments to be made in the interim) if HMRC are satisfied that the conditions will be met within prerequisite time limits.

Law: ITA 2007, s. 274

9.2.1 Summary of conditions

The conditions that must be met in the company's most recent accounting period (and must be expected to be met in the period in which the approval is requested) are set out at ITA 2007, s. 274. The table is reproduced (with internal links) in the *Venture Capital Schemes Manual* at VCM 54020. The table as it appears in the legislation is:

Description	Condition
The listing condition	The shares making up the company's ordinary share capital (or, if there are such shares of more than one class, those of each class) have been or will be admitted to trading on a regulated market throughout the relevant period.
The nature of income condition	The company's income in the relevant period has been or will be derived wholly or mainly from shares or securities.
The income retention condition	The company has not retained or will not retain an amount which is greater than 15% of the income it derived or will derive in the relevant period from shares or securities.
The 15% holding limit condition	No holding in any company, other than a VCT or a company that would qualify as a VCT but for the listing condition, has represented or will represent at any time during the relevant period more than 15% by value of the company's investments.
The 80% qualifying holdings condition	At least 80% by value of the company's investments has been or will be represented throughout the relevant period by shares or securities included in qualifying holdings of the company [see note 1].
The 70% eligible shares condition	At least 70% by value of the company's qualifying holdings has been or will be represented throughout the relevant period by holdings of eligible shares.
The non-qualifying investments condition	The company has not made and will not make, in the relevant period, an investment which is neither of the following [see note 2]: a) an investment that on the date it is made is included in the company's qualifying holdings; b) an investment as described in **9.2.11** below.

Description	Condition
The investment limits condition	The company has not made and will not make an investment, in the relevant period, in a company which breaches the permitted investment limits.
The minimum investment on further issue condition (post FA 2018)	The company has not breached and will not breach, in the relevant period, the minimum investment on further issue condition [see note 2].
The permitted maximum age condition	The company has not made and will not make an investment, in the relevant period, in a company which breaches the permitted maximum age limit.
The no business acquisition condition	The company has not made and will not make an investment, in the relevant period, in a company which breaches the prohibition on business acquisitions.

Each of these conditions is considered in turn below.

Notes

1. Increase from 70% to 80% from a date to be appointed under FA 2018, Sch. 5, para. 13.
2. New conditions imposed from a date to be appointed under FA 2018, Sch. 5, para. 13.

Law: ITA 2007, s. 274
Guidance: VCM 54020

9.2.2 The listing condition

The ordinary share capital VCT must be traded on an EU regulated market from 6 April 2011. An EU regulated market is one which the relevant competent authority recognises as meeting the Commission's definition of a regulated market. In the UK this is the responsibility of the Financial Services Authority (FSA).

The Commission publishes and updates a list of all currently recognised regulated markets, and a link to the current version is given at the end of this subsection. There are currently seven recognised regulated markets in the UK; including the London stock exchange, EDX, and ICE Futures Europe.

Law: ITA 2007, s. 274

9.2.3 The nature of income condition

A VCT's income must derive wholly or mainly from shares or securities. This condition will be regarded as met if at least 70% of the VCT's income derives from such sources. There are specific rules in relation to loan relationships. The income taken into account for the purposes of this condition should exclude any of the company's debtor relationships. In respect of non-trading loan relationships, the amount to be brought into consideration as income should be the excess of credits over debits.

Law: ITA 2007, s. 276

9.2.4 The income retention condition

A VCT is not permitted to retain more than 15% of the gross income it receives from shares and securities. Such monies are therefore required to be extinguished in the ordinary course of business, whether by investment in qualifying companies or otherwise.

Dividends declared in respect of an accounting period do not count as retained income, provided that they are declared before the date that the accounts are drawn up.

There is a *de minimis* let out from applying this condition where the retained income does not exceed £10,000 for an accounting period of 12 months (or a proportionally reduced amount for shorter accounting periods). There is a further partial disapplication in cases where the company is required by law to retain more than 15% of its income.

Law: ITA 2007, s. 276

9.2.5 The 15% holding limit condition

A VCT is prevented from avoiding diversification of investments, as it is not permitted to invest an amount that is greater than 15% of its entire investment base in any single company (or collectively in any group of companies). This includes all classes of shares in a company, and so where an investor holds different share classes (e.g. A shares and B shares), these are pooled together when considering the 15% test.

The condition will not be considered as being breached if the 15% test was met at the time the particular shares were acquired, or the most recent time that the holding was added to (the consideration). The condition will be treated as being continued to be satisfied until the next addition to the holding. This prevents the condition from being breached simply because (for example) other shareholdings are disposed of, increasing the relative share by reference to the investment base.

Law: ITA 2007, s. 277-279

9.2.6 The 80% qualifying holdings condition

A VCT's investment base must consist of a minimum of 80% of investments in qualifying holdings. This condition must be met throughout its most recent accounting period for approval to continue.

When a shareholding is disposed of, any effect the disposal has on meeting the 80% test is disregarded (in most circumstances – but see VCM 54100 for exceptions) for a period of six months; giving the VCT time to reinvest the funds and ensure that the condition continues to be met.

Qualifying holdings are not considered in depth in this publication, as it is a concern for VCT managers rather than investors. Broadly speaking, a shareholding will be qualifying if it is made into an EIS type company; and indeed the restrictions placed on the VCT by the relevant legislation as to what it can invest in closely follow the EIS restrictions – including the FA 2016 exclusion of all energy-generation activities.

Anyone seeking further detail regarding qualifying holdings for these purposes should refer to the legislation contained in ITA 2007, Pt. 6, Ch. 4 and the *Venture Capital Schemes Manual* at VCM 55000 onwards.

Note that prior to enactment of *Finance Act* 2018, the qualifying holdings had to make up 70% of the total holdings.

Law: ITA 2007, Pt. 6, Ch. 4
Guidance: VCM 55000ff.

9.2.7 The 70% eligible shares condition

From 6 April 2011, the VCT is required to ensure that at least 70% of the VCT's qualifying holdings consist of eligible shares. These are defined by TCGA 1992, s. 285 as those which do not carry:

- present or future rights to the company's assets upon a winding up;
- present or future redemption rights; or
- present or future rights to preferential variable or cumulative dividends.

For the purposes of this test, the value of the qualifying holdings means the value when acquired, or (if applicable) when the most recent addition was made to the holding. Different share classes are not aggregated for the purposes of this test, and so ordinary shares must be looked at separately from other classes of shares, and acquisitions of new classes do not affect the value of ordinary shares already acquired.

There is a restricted relaxation of this test in circumstances where a VCT issues new shares in order to raise money for a specified purpose.

Law: TCGA 1992, s. 285

9.2.8 The investment limits condition

The maximum amount a VCT can invest in a single company in any 12 month period is restricted to £5 million, mirroring the EIS conditions and reflecting the fact that VCTs are (in the main) restricted to investing in EIS type companies.

When considering the £5 million limit, any amounts that the investee company has received via EIS, SEIS, other VCTs, and any other EU approved State aid type funding in the year must be included. The limit is therefore in practice a restriction applied to the investee company, and from the VCT's point of view is merely a hypothetical maximum.

From April 2016, investments as described in s. 274(3A) (see **9.2.11** below) are not included in references to "investments" for these purposes.

Law: ITA 2007, s. 274(3A), 280B

9.2.9 The permitted maximum age condition

This condition was imposed by F(No.2)A 2015, with effect from 18 November 2015. The condition broadly restricts the VCT from investing in more established companies, in the same way that changes made at the same time to the EIS legislation prevent individuals from doing so. Refer to **4.2.6** for further details on the restriction.

From April 2016, investments as described in s. 274(3A) (see **9.2.11** below) are not included in references to "investments" for these purposes.

Law: ITA 2007, s. 274(3A), 280C

9.2.10 The no business acquisition condition

Another new condition introduced with effect from 18 November 2015 (again mirroring changes made to the EIS legislation) is that the investee company must not employ the funds raised by the VCT's investment for the purposes of acquiring:

- an interest in another company such that a company becomes a 51% subsidiary of the relevant company;
- a further interest in a company which is a 51% subsidiary of the relevant company;
- a trade;
- intangible assets employed for the purposes of a trade; or
- goodwill employed for the purposes of a trade.

A VCT making an investment into a company which breaches this use of money raised condition will fail to meet the conditions for approval.

From April 2016, investments as described in s. 274(3A) (see **9.2.11** below) are not included in references to "investments" for these purposes.

Law: ITA 2007, s. 274(3A), 280D

9.2.11 Non-qualifying investments

Finance Act 2016 introduced a new condition applicable to investments made on or after 6 April 2016. The condition is that the company has not made and will not make, in the relevant period, an investment which is neither of the following:

(a) an investment that on the date it is made is included in the company's qualifying holdings;

(b) an investment as described in new subsection 3A of s. 274.

The investments fall within s. 274(3A) if they are any of the following:

(a) shares or units in an AIF (within the meaning given by reg. 3 of the *Alternative Investment Fund Managers Regulations* 2013) which may be repurchased or redeemed on seven days' notice given by the investor;

(b) shares or units in a UCITS (within the meaning given by s. 363A(4) of TIOPA 2010) which may be repurchased or redeemed on seven days' notice given by the investor;

(c) ordinary shares or securities in a company which are acquired by the investor on a regulated market;

(d) money in the investor's possession;

(e) a sum owed to the investor which:

- under s. 285(4)(b) (read with s. 285(5) and (6)) is to be regarded as an investment of the investor; and
- is such that the investor's right mentioned in s. 285(5)(a) may be exercised on seven days' notice given by the investor.

Law: ITA 2007, s. 274(3A)

9.2.12 Minimum investment on further issue

Finance Act 2018 introduces a new restriction that requires a VCT that has issued share capital to invest at least 30% of the money raised by a subsequent share issue into qualifying shares or securities within twelve months of the end of the accounting period in which the later share issue took place.

Law: ITA 2007, s. 280BA

9.3 Provisional approval

Where the conditions required for full approval discussed in **9.2** have not been met in the most recent accounting period, provisional approval may be given if the prospective VCT can satisfy HMRC that they will shortly be met, and continue to be so met.

The relevant period for which the prospective VCT must satisfy HMRC as to this varies from condition to condition. This is clearly set out in VCM 54030, which is partially reproduced below:

> "A company which does not meet the conditions for full approval (see VCM54020) may be given provisional approval where it satisfies HMRC that:
>
> - in relation to the current accounting period and future accounting periods:
>   - it has not made and will not make an investment in a company, which breaches the permitted investment limit
> - in relation to the accounting period which is current when the application is made and future accounting periods:
>   - its income will be derived wholly or mainly from shares or securities (VCM54050),
>   - no holding in any company will represent more than 15% by value of its investments at any time (VCM54200),
>   - its ordinary share capital will be included in the official UK list throughout. From 6 April 2011 the ordinary share capital of a VCT no longer has to be included in the official UK list. The condition becomes that it must be admitted to trading on a regulated market in accordance with Directive 2004/39/EC of the European Parliament (see VCM54030), and

        - it will not retain more than 15% of its income derived in them from shares and securities (see VCM54210).
- in relation to an accounting period of the company beginning no more than 3 years after approval is given or, if earlier, when approval takes effect, and in following accounting periods:
    - at least 70% by value of its investments will be in qualifying holdings of shares or securities throughout (VCM54060 onwards),
    - at least 30% by value of its qualifying holdings will be in holdings of eligible shares throughout (VCM54110).
    - from 6 April 2011 at least 70% by value of its qualifying holdings will be in holdings of eligible shares throughout (VCM54110)."

HMRC may impose additional conditions which, in their opinion, will ensure that the above conditions are likely to be met. Failure to make such conditions may see provisional approval being withdrawn at a later date.

Law: ITA 2007, s. 275
Guidance: VCM 54030

9.4 Withdrawal of approval

Once approval is given, it can be withdrawn at a later date where there are reasonable grounds for believing that:

- the conditions for approval were not actually met at the time the approval was given;
- when HMRC were satisfied that the condition would be met in a particular period, it transpires that the condition will not or was not met in the period;
- an additional condition set out when giving provisional approval has not been met;
- following full approval, any required condition was not met or will not be met in respect of the company's latest or current accounting period; or

- where there has been a further issue of ordinary shares, the conditions for approval will not be met in the first accounting period in which the relaxation does not apply.

The effect of a withdrawal of approval on individual investors is discussed in subsequent chapters.

Law: ITA 2007, s. 281

10. Income tax relief

10.1 Overview

A qualifying investment in VCT shares offers both front end income tax relief, and ongoing relief for dividends paid in respect of the shares. We will consider the qualifying conditions in relation to the investor and the investment in this chapter.

10.2 Front end tax relief

10.2.1 Detail of relief

The relief is given as a bottom line income tax reducer, taking priority over relief for EIS investments, calculated as the lower of:

- an amount equal to tax at 30% on amounts subscribed within the "permitted maximum"; and
- the amount which reduces the individual's income tax liability to £nil.

The front end income tax relief can only be claimed by those who subscribe for new shares. The permitted maximum is £200,000. In order to preserve the relief, the investor must hold the shares continuously for at least 5 years from the date of the investment.

Unlike EIS/SEIS/SITR there is no facility to carry back relief to the prior tax year, and so the limit is absolute in this regard – if shares in excess of £200,000 are subscribed for, no relief can be claimed on the excess. This is also applicable when considering the dividend and CGT exemptions. It is vital to keep a record of the order of share purchases in order to identify correctly which shares attract relief.

Example – part qualifying investment

During 2018-19, Morgan makes the following investments into qualifying VCTs (all for £1 per share):

1. 6 April 2018 – 150,000 shares in A Ltd.
2. 1 July 2018 – 60,000 further shares in A Ltd.
3. 1 December 2018 – 20,000 shares in B Ltd.

He is entitled to claim VCT relief of 30% on the whole of the first investment, and on 50,000 of the second investment. The remaining 10,000 shares, and the entire investment into B Ltd, do not attract any income tax relief – and will not enjoy dividend tax exemption or CGT exemption either.

Relief is attributable to shares acquired earlier in priority to shares acquired later on.

In the example above, without adequate record keeping, the shares in (for example) B Ltd may be sold completely separately from the other shares, at a gain. This would be taxable; however this will not be apparent unless the accountant (or investor) remembers, and so the CGT exemption may be erroneously assumed to apply. This could lead to a later assessment, and penalties.

Law: ITA 2007, s. 262, 263

10.2.2 Who can claim?

The restrictions on investors are far less onerous than the equivalent under the EIS legislation. Broadly, anyone aged 18 or older can invest and claim the relief, provided the shares are new ordinary shares, paid up in cash at the time of the investment.

The shares must not carry any present or future rights to:

- dividends;
- rights to the assets of the VCT in the event of a winding up; or
- redemption.

There are, however, some specific anti-avoidance provisions to consider.

Law: ITA 2007, s. 261

10.2.3 No tax avoidance

No relief can be given if the shares were not acquired for a genuine commercial purpose, or were acquired as part of a scheme or arrangement the main purpose (or one of the main purposes) of which is the avoidance of tax.

Law: ITA 2007, s. 261(3)

10.2.4 No linked loans

Relief is not available if, during the relevant period, the investor receives a loan which in the absence of an investment:

- would not have been made; or
- would not have been made on the same terms.

Any loan that can be linked to the shares issued will fall foul of the rules, where this would not have been made – or would not have been made on the same terms – without the investment taking place.

Section 264(2) of ITA 2007 extends the meaning of "loan" for these purposes to include the extension of credit to the investor (or his associates), and assignment of debts due from the investor (or his associates).

The relevant period is that which begins with:

- the incorporation of the company; or (if later)
- the date two years before the issue of the shares,

and ends immediately before the fifth anniversary of that issue.

Law: ITA 2007, s. 264

10.2.5 Linked sales

No relief can be given if the shares are subscribed for under arrangements involving a "linked sale". This provision is intended to prevent recycling of VCT relief via share buy back arrangements.

Example – recycling relief

Miriam bought shares in VCT Ltd in 2013-14. In 2018-19, after the fifth anniversary of the investment, the VCT offers to buy back the shares, providing she reinvests the proceeds back into the VCT.

Prior to 6 April 2014, the situation described in the example would see the original relief claimed (in 2013-14) preserved, and a fresh amount of relief available in 2018-19 for the new investment. FA 2014 introduced a specific counter measure to address this.

If an investment is subject to a linked sale, then the consideration figure used in calculating the relief due is reduced by the proceeds received (or by the amount that reduces it to £nil) for the linked sale of other shares.

Where there is more than one new investment linked to a sale, the reduction discussed above is applied to the earlier investment first.

A sale is "linked" for the purposes of this provision if:

- an individual has sold shares in the same VCT as the one in which he subscribed for shares, or in a VCT which is treated as a successor or predecessor of that VCT; and
- either the subscription for shares is in some way conditionally linked with the share sale, or the subscription and sale are within six months of each other.

Where an investor elects to utilise dividends to purchase further shares, this is not caught by this provision.

Finance Act 2018 amended this rule slightly to relax its application in the event of certain mergers. This has retrospective effect for all share issues on or after 6 April 2014.

Now, the rule only applies to a share subscription where:

- it is to a VCT that has previously merged; or
- it is made less than two years before the VCT merges and where either the investor knows the merger is to take place, or the merger is an arrangement intended to confer a tax advantage to the VCT investors.

For these purposes, the date of a merger is the date of the share issue, or first share issue if there is more than one.

Law: ITA 2007, s. 264A; FA 2018, Sch. 5, para. 1

10.2.6 Risk to capital

Finance Act 2018 contains a new condition for investments to ensure that they are made at full risk to the investor's capital. The new provision is included as s. 286ZA.

For investments made on or after 15 March 2018 (the date specified in the original tax policy note), relief will only be given if, at the time of the investment, it is reasonable to conclude that both:

- the investee company has an objective to grow and develop its trade in the long term; and
- there is a significant risk that the investor could lose more of the capital invested than he or she gets back by way of other returns from the investment.

The second condition means that investments that have little or no probability of anything but small movements in value – say plus or minus 10% – might not qualify as this is far lower than the 30% income tax relief.

The condition will be assessed giving due consideration and regard to any circumstances existing at the time of the investment. The new s. 286ZA(3) sets out a non-exhaustive list of circumstances that will be considered:

(a) the extent to which the company's objectives include increasing the number of its employees or the turnover of its trade;

(b) the nature of the company's sources of income, including the extent to which there is a significant risk of the company not receiving some or all of the income;

(c) the extent to which the company has or is likely to have assets, or is or could become a party to arrangements for acquiring assets, that could be used to secure financing from any person;

(d) the extent to which the activities of the company are subcontracted to persons who are not connected with it;

(e) the nature of the company's ownership structure or management structure, including the extent to which others participate in or devise the structure;

(f) how any opportunity for investment in the company is marketed; and

(g) the extent to which arrangements are in place under which opportunities for investments in the company are or may be marketed with, or otherwise associated with, opportunities for investments in other companies or entities.

Law: ITA 2007, s. 286ZA

10.3 Withdrawal of front end tax relief

Once relief is given, there are a number of circumstances where it may be withdrawn or reduced.

Law: ITA 2007, s. 266

10.3.1 Early disposal of shares

Relief will be reduced, up to the full amount of the original income tax reduction, where the investor disposes of the shares before the fifth anniversary of the investment – other than where the disposal is to a spouse or civil partner with whom the investor is living at the time of the disposal.

If the shares were disposed of to a spouse or civil partner, and that recipient then disposes of the shares before the fifth anniversary of the investment, any reduction in relief is assessable on the recipient and not the original investor.

Where there are multiple holdings, shares acquired earlier are treated as being disposed of first. Where shares acquired on the same day only partially qualify for relief (for example where there is an excessive investment) the shares to which no relief is attributable are treated as being disposed of before shares on which relief has been claimed.

The reduction in relief given is calculated by reference to the sales proceeds and the original rate of relief, but restricted to the amount of relief given on the shares. The reduction is therefore the lower of:

- sales proceeds x VCT relief rate (30%); or
- the relief attributable to the shares.

Example – reduction

Owain subscribes for new VCT shares on 6 April 2018. He pays £100,000 for 100,000 shares, claiming £30,000 of VCT relief. On 7 May 2018, he sells 40,000 shares for £34,000. The relief which must be withdrawn is the lower of:

- 34,000 x 30% = £10,200; and
- £30,000 x (40,000/100,000) = £12,000

Therefore Owain's relief is reduced by £10,200.

Note that the £1,800 that is not withdrawn (due to the fall in share value) becomes permanent, because the shares are no longer held.

If the shares are disposed of otherwise than by a bargain made at arm's-length, the relief is not reduced but withdrawn in full regardless of the level of proceeds. For example, if an investor in VCT shares knowingly disposes of them for less than their market value, all the upfront relief will be withdrawn.

Law: ITA 2007, s. 266, 267

10.3.2 VCT loses approval

An investor can also lose his or her front-end income tax relief if the VCT company loses its approved status. Withdrawal of approval of a VCT immediately leads to any shareholders who have claimed VCT relief being treated as if they have made a disposal of the shares otherwise than for a bargain at arm's-length. If the withdrawal takes place before the fifth anniversary of the investment, the relief will be fully withdrawn as a result.

Law: ITA 2007, s. 268

10.3.3 Relief found not to have been due

If it transpires that relief was given, but should not have been, HMRC can raise an assessment to recover it.

Law: ITA 2007, s. 269

10.3.4 Assessments

All assessments for the recovery of relief which has been reduced or withdrawn must be made for the tax year in which the relief was claimed, and not the year in which the event leading to the withdrawal or reduction occurred. The time limit for making such an assessment is six years from the end of the tax year in which the relief was claimed. An individual must notify HMRC within 60 days upon becoming aware of circumstances arising which mean that relief must be withdrawn or reduced.

Law: ITA 2007, s. 270

10.4 Dividend tax exemption

10.4.1 Giving the exemption

Where an individual aged 18 or over acquires VCT shares up to the permitted maximum, any dividends paid on the shares whilst the VCT remains approved are exempt from tax.

The individual does not have to subscribe for new shares. VCT shares are traded on regulated markets and so it is relatively easy to come by second-hand shares. The second-hand shares cannot attract income tax relief, which can only be claimed once in respect of the same shares, but the dividend tax exemption is freely available, provided the shares were bought for genuine commercial purposes.

In cases where shares with more than £200,000 are acquired in the tax year, the dividend exemption is restricted to the first £200,000 of shares bought, in a similar way to the restriction on front-end income tax relief discussed above.

Exempt dividends do not need to be reported on the tax return – i.e. the relief is automatic and does not need to be claimed. Prior to 6 April 2016, dividends carried a notional tax credit. These could not be used to offset income tax liability insofar as they related to exempt VCT dividends.

VCT shares often form a substantial part of a managed investment portfolio. It is crucial when preparing the income tax return to check whether qualifying VCT dividends have been accounted for properly, that is to say they have been left out of the consolidated income statement which is produced for tax purposes. If not then a manual adjustment will need to be made.

Law: ITTOIA 2005, s. 709, 710

10.4.2 Withdrawal of relief

Dividends are only exempt as long as the VCT retains its approved status. If the VCT had received full approval, but this is subsequently withdrawn, any dividends paid after the withdrawal date will be fully taxable.

If the VCT approval was only provisional, and this is removed because (for example) some condition of the provisional approval was not met, the VCT is treated as never having been approved. In these circumstances, therefore, any dividends paid during the period of provisional approval will need to be taxed.

Law: ITA 2007, s. 281

10.5 Claiming relief

There is no obligation for a VCT to issue an income tax relief certificate; however if an investor asks for one the VCT must issue this within 30 days. There is some specific information that such a certificate should show, though there is no prescribed format:

- the name and permanent address of the investor;
- the date on which the shares were issued;
- the amounts paid and the date they were received; and
- details of any amounts outstanding in the case of partly paid shares.

The certificate should certify that the shares issued were eligible shares and that, to the best of the VCT's knowledge, the shares were issued for genuine commercial purposes and not for the avoidance of tax, and that there were no linked loans in existence which would disqualify the investor from relief.

The investor is (at least in theory) not required to submit the certificate when making a claim, either via the tax return or as a stand-alone claim, unless the officer processing it has reason to doubt its authenticity. In practice, however, it is prudent to send the certificate if making a stand-alone claim, or requesting an amendment to the PAYE code, to reduce any delays.

It is common practice for most VCTs to produce and send income tax relief certificates at the same time as the share certificates following investment.

If the claim is being made on the tax return, the investor should complete the appropriate box on the additional information pages (SA101). If requesting an amendment to a PAYE code, or requesting a refund via a stand-alone claim, this should be done in writing to the appropriate tax office.

Law: SI 1995/1979, reg. 9

11. CGT disposal relief

11.1 Overview

This section considers when the CGT exemption applies for gains on shares held in a qualifying VCT.

Where shares were acquired before 6 April 2004, it was also possible to claim CGT deferral relief on qualifying investments. Because this facility was removed, it is not discussed in this publication. Advisers do, however, need to be aware of the potential for deferred gains coming back into charge, and so should familiarise themselves with the relevant sections of Schedule 5C to TCGA 1992, and HMRC guidance at VCM 53090 etc. accordingly.

Law: TCGA 1992, s. 151A

11.2 The exemption

Gains made on the sale of ordinary shares in VCTs are not chargeable where certain conditions are met. Neither can losses be offset against other gains or income.

Law: TCGA 1992, s. 151A(1), (2)

11.2.1 Conditions

The conditions which must be met are that the company the shares were held in:

- was a Venture Capital Trust at the time the shares were acquired; and
- was a Venture Capital Trust at the time the shares were disposed,

and the disposal was a "qualifying disposal".

A disposal is a qualifying disposal if:

- it is made by a person who is at least 18 years old;
- it is made in respect of shares that were not acquired in excess of the permitted annual maximum; and

- the individual acquired the shares for bona fide commercial reasons, and not as part of a scheme in which one of the main intentions was the avoidance of tax.

Shares do not have to have been subscribed for in order to qualify for the CGT exemption, so shares acquired second-hand from another person can qualify subject to the permitted annual maximum condition.

Law: TCGA 1992, s. 151A(1), (2)

11.2.2 Partially eligible disposals

It may transpire that there is a disposal of shares in a VCT, and that the individual holds some shares that are eligible but others that are non-eligible for the CGT exemption. This may occur where:

- shares are acquired in excess of the permitted annual maximum; or
- shares are acquired before the VCT receives approval.

Shares are again treated as being disposed on a first-in first-out basis. Where both qualifying and non-qualifying shares were acquired on the same day, the non-qualifying shares are treated as being disposed of first.

To demonstrate this let's reconsider the example of Morgan from the previous chapter.

Example – part qualifying investment

During 2016-17, Morgan made the following investments into qualifying VCTs (all for £1 per share):

1. 6 April 2016 – 150,000 shares in A Ltd.
2. 1 July 2016 – 60,000 further shares in A Ltd.
3. 1 December 2016 – 20,000 shares in B Ltd.

Morgan sells all the shares in January 2022. He is entitled to claim CGT exemption on the whole of the first investment, and on 50,000 shares of the second investment. The remaining 10,000 shares in A Ltd, and the entire investment into B Ltd, do not attract CGT exemption.

Guidance: VCM 52040

11.2.3 Share identification

The ordinary share matching and pooling rules do not apply to shares acquired in a VCT that qualify for VCT relief. Share identification of mixed holdings is discussed below.

Two sets of identification rules are in fact required. Firstly, rules are applied to determine if any shares were acquired in excess of the permitted annual maximum. Secondly, identification rules are applied on the disposal to determine whether it is the qualifying or non-qualifying shares which have been disposed of.

Permitted maximum

The identification rules are identical to the ones for identifying qualifying shares for the purpose of attributing income tax relief. For clarification:

- shares acquired earlier in the year are treated as acquired for the purposes of VCT relief before shares acquired later (i.e. the investor cannot specify which shares relief applies to);
- where shares are acquired on the same day, and the total value of all VCT shares on that day causes the maximum permitted amount to be exceeded, relief is attributable on a proportionate basis – by reference to the market value of all shares acquired on that day.

Example – attribution of relief

Ian has already acquired £175,000 of qualifying VCT1 Ltd shares in 2018-19. On 1 March 2019 he acquires £30,000 worth of shares in VCT1 Ltd and £20,000 worth in VCT2 Ltd – both are approved VCTs. To determine which shares the relief applies to, an apportionment must be made:

Relief attributable to VCT1 =

$$£25{,}000 \text{ x } \frac{£30{,}000}{£50{,}000} = £15{,}000$$

Relief attributable to VCT2 =

$$£25{,}000 \text{ x } \frac{£20{,}000}{£50{,}000} = £10{,}000$$

Therefore the £25,000 of permitted investment is allocated accordingly.

Disposal identification rules

Upon a disposal, there may be shares which have been acquired in excess of the permitted annual maximum as discussed above. Where this is the case, further identification rules are required. Shares which are eligible for VCT relief do not follow the share pooling rules contained in TCGA 1992, s. 104 but are instead subject to specific rules. Shares are treated as being disposed of in the following order:

- first, any shares which were acquired prior to the VCT obtaining approved status; and
- next, any other shares acquired on a first-in first-out basis.

For the purposes of determining the order of shares acquired on the same day, shares to which relief is *not* attributable are treated as being disposed of before shares to which relief is attributable.

Example – Ian continued

On 1 April 2024, Ian disposes of shares in VCT1 Ltd with a base cost of £195,000. The shares disposed of are identified as:

- £175,000 (original cost) being acquired earliest in the year;
- £15,000 (original cost) acquired on 1 March 2019, and not qualifying for relief (see above); and
- £5,000 (original cost) acquired on 1 March 2019 and qualifying for relief.

The disposal will therefore see shares costing £15,000 falling to be charged to CGT, and therefore there may be a tax bill depending on the proceeds and availability of the annual exemption.

Law: TCGA 1992, s. 151A(4), (5), 151B

11.2.4 Share reorganisations

Where there is a reorganisation of share capital within the meaning of TCGA 1992, s. 126 (rights issues, etc.), special rules can also apply. Essentially these only apply where there is a mixed holding of shares – that is where there are shares held in a VCT that are in at least two of the following categories:

- eligible for both CGT disposal relief and income tax relief;
- only eligible for CGT disposal relief;
- only eligible for income tax relief;
- not eligible for either relief.

The shares in each category are treated as separate holdings, and then identified with a new separate holding for the purposes of TCGA 1992, s. 127. In practice this will mean an apportionment between the applicable categories.

Example – bonus issue

Shirley holds 150,000 shares in VCT Ltd.

Of these, 100,000 were subscribed for and attracted income tax relief and are eligible for CGT disposal relief.

The other 50,000 shares were purchased second hand from another investor, and so are not eligible for front end income tax relief.

The company issues a 1 for 2 bonus issue – and Jane receives 75,000 shares accordingly. 50,000 shares are allotted to the 100,000 shares qualifying for both reliefs, and the remaining 25,000 are allotted to the 50,000 second hand shares. The base cost of the increased holding does not change, but the marginal base cost is diluted.

The normal no-acquisition no-disposal rule does not apply where the reorganisation results in new shares being acquired for money. Instead, the new shareholdings are treated as a separate acquisition, and so the eligibility for VCT reliefs will depend on the annual maximum not being exceeded in the tax year in which the reorganisation takes place. The original shareholdings are not affected.

Law: TCGA 1992, s. 126, 127

11.3 Loss of VCT approval

The effect of a loss of approval depends on whether the approval was full or provisional.

If the approval was only provisional, its removal will mean that the VCT is never treated as having been approved, and so any disposals that have happened prior to the date the approval is removed will need to be assessed for CGT retrospectively.

If the approval was full, then any disposals that occurred prior to the date that the approval was removed, and that were exempt, will not be affected; however any disposals after that date will no longer enjoy the exemption.

As a practical point, this will be the case even if the shares were held for more than five years and the income tax relief was therefore secured. This is because (unlike EIS relief) there is a specific requirement for the company to be a VCT at the date of the disposal.

A deemed disposal (for the purposes of VCT relief) occurs when there is a loss of approval (as discussed in **10.3.2**). It follows that if a VCT which loses approval subsequently regains it, the entitlement to CGT exemption is not renewed, because the trigger event (the deemed disposal) determining the loss of relief has already happened.

Law: TCGA 1992, s. 151B(6), (7)

Seed Enterprise Investment Scheme

12. Introduction and background

12.1 History

The Seed Enterprise Investment Scheme (SEIS) is relatively new. It was introduced from 6 April 2012. The stated aim of the scheme was linked to boosting economic growth by promoting new enterprises to potential outside investors, via generous tax reliefs.

The SEIS can be thought of as the EIS in miniature; specifically introduced to help the very small new businesses to attract capital finance. Following the 2008 banking crisis, many banks around the world were saved by government bailouts, including in the UK. In the ensuing years, banks were particularly reluctant to lend money to small, new and unproven businesses, largely because of irresponsible lending which had contributed to the crisis.

Despite efforts by the UK government to lean on banks to encourage them to be accommodating to entrepreneurs, and specifically earmarked funds made available by the government in the way of grants and subsidies, new businesses were still struggling to get off the ground.

The SEIS was intended to encourage investors to take a risk on these new businesses. In practice, the overall impact of SEIS is small in comparison to the main EIS; however often an investment attracts, or can attract, both SEIS and EIS relief if structured correctly.

Law: TCGA 1992, s. 150E, Sch. 5BB; ITA 2007, Pt. 5A

12.2 Restricted

The SEIS is available to far fewer companies than the main EIS. There are greater restrictions in terms of the age of the trade, employee numbers, gross assets etc., and the inherent risk associated with the share investment is consequently higher than the main EIS. Ordinarily this would mean a far less attractive prospective investment, and so the tax relief available through SEIS is correspondingly greater than EIS.

12.3 Summary of tax reliefs

12.3.1 Overview

There are three specific aspects of SEIS:

- income tax relief;
- capital gains tax (CGT) exemption; and
- CGT reinvestment relief.

There is no specific provision for SEIS shares to qualify for "share loss relief" – i.e. to be able to offset capital losses against general income. However, in most cases, SEIS shares will qualify for the relief under the general provisions of ITA 2007, s. 131 in any case. Losses are discussed in the CGT disposal relief section.

Law: ITA 2007, s. 131

12.3.2 Income tax relief

Subject to the qualifying conditions, SEIS income tax relief is given at the rate of 50% of the amount invested in the qualifying company up to a maximum of £100,000 per investor per tax year. As for EIS, this is restricted if the individual's income tax liability for the particular year is lower than 50% of the investment. The tax relief cannot reduce the tax liability below £nil.

Example – Deiniol

Deiniol makes a qualifying investment into an SEIS company on 6 April 2018. He invests the maximum amount of £100,000. The maximum SEIS income tax relief available is £50,000; however his income tax liability for the year is only £40,000. He can therefore claim relief of £40,000 in his income tax return.

An investor can elect to carry back some or all of the investment into the tax year immediately preceding the year of investment. This can be useful where relief cannot be claimed in full in the year of investment, due to an insufficient income tax liability. So in the example above the investor could look to carry back £20,000 of the investment into 2017-18 – provided he had an income tax liability to offset in that year.

Law: ITA 2007, s. 257AB

12.3.3 CGT exemption

Where a claim to SEIS income tax relief has been made and not subsequently withdrawn, any gain arising on the SEIS shares themselves will not be charged to CGT upon a disposal. It is often not appreciated that any gain deferred will come back into charge in the year of the disposal.

The exemption is affected by any reduction in income tax relief. As for EIS relief, a claim for income tax relief must have actually been made for the exemption to apply.

Law: TCGA 1992, s. 150A

12.3.4 CGT reinvestment relief

This relief is unique to the SEIS. It is similar to the EIS deferral relief; however under SEIS, no amount of gain is deferred. Instead, up to 50% of a gain matched to a qualifying SEIS investment can be completely exempted from CGT.

Example – Holly

Holly makes a chargeable gain of £90,000 on 1 May 2018. On 1 January 2019, she makes a qualifying SEIS investment of £100,000. Holly can claim reinvestment relief on 50% of the chargeable gain. £45,000 of the gain is therefore exempt from CGT, subject to qualifying conditions.

Where an investment was made in 2012-13, 100% of the matched gains could be exempted. This may be important for practitioners to be aware of, because the time limits for making a claim is five years from the tax return filing deadline, i.e. 31 January 2019 for the 2012-13 tax year.

Where a carryback claim is made for income tax relief purposes, the appropriate rate at which capital gains are potentially exempted follows the year the income tax relief is given for, not the actual year of investment. If, therefore, an investor makes a qualifying investment in 2013-14, making a claim for income tax relief to be carried back to 2012-13 could lead to a higher CGT exemption.

Law: TCGA 1992, Sch. 5BB

12.4 Claiming relief

The issuing company must first complete form SEIS1 - the compliance statement - with the relevant details about itself, the nature of its business, and the investments to which SEIS relief is intended to apply. HMRC will then consider the application, and provided the tax officer is happy that all qualifying conditions are satisfied HMRC will issue the company with authority to issue SEIS certificates to each of the investors. It will enclose blank SEIS3 certificates to enable this.

The company will then need to complete the certificates, and issue these to the relevant investors. The investors can then claim tax relief, either on their individual tax returns or by contacting the PAYE office to give effect to relief via their tax codes.

Note that relief cannot be claimed until the certificates are issued.

It is often the case that investors will seek relief under both SEIS and EIS for substantially the same investment by splitting the issue into two tranches - i.e. SEIS relief on the first £100,000, and EIS relief on everything else. This is fine provided that the SEIS shares are issued first; however, the Tribunal cases of *X-Wind Power Limited* and *GDR Food Technology Limited* have established that relief cannot be given where the EIS1 form is mistakenly filled out instead. One of the conditions for SEIS relief is that there have been no shares issued under EIS, and so once an EIS3 compliance statement is issued, the opportunity to claim SEIS relief is lost - even if the EIS form is completed in error.

Law: ITA 2007, s. 257EC, 257ED

Cases: *X-Wind Power Ltd v HMRC* [2016] UKFTT 317 (TC); *GDR Food Technology Ltd v HMRC* [2016] UKFTT 466 (TC)

13. Income tax relief: investor conditions

13.1 Overview

The investor is the person who purchases shares in a company. The decision to do this may be partly influenced by the possibility of SEIS relief. Note that the investor does not have to be a serial investor, and the SEIS shares could be his or her very first investment.

The investor may be required to complete a declaration that he is either a certified high net worth individual, or a self-certified "sophisticated investor". However, neither of these is a formal requirement for qualifying for SEIS relief; rather they are requirements to safeguard investors who make high-risk or alternative investments.

The requirements that an investor must meet before qualifying for SEIS income tax relief are contained within Chapter 2 of Part 5A of ITA 2007. All references given below are therefore to this statute, unless otherwise stated. Before looking at the conditions in detail, it is worthwhile spending some time becoming familiar with the various periods and dates referred to in the legislation, as these are referred to frequently throughout.

The investor needs to be an individual, but there is no requirement that he must be UK resident or domiciled. He would, however, need a UK income tax liability to take advantage of the income tax relief. Trustees cannot claim the income tax relief, though the beneficiary of a bare trust or nominee arrangement could.

Law: ITA 2007, Pt. 5A, Ch. 2

13.2 Periods and key dates

13.2.1 Periods A and B

Some of the qualifying conditions need to be met only at the time of investment; however, some need to be met for periods beginning before the investment date, and/or afterwards.

Under SEIS, there are only two time periods discussed in the relevant legislation:

1. Period A – beginning with either the incorporation date and ending immediately before the "termination date" of the relevant shares (see **13.2.2** below).
2. Period B – beginning with the share issue date, and ending immediately before the termination date.

It is important to recognise the difference between Period A and Period B, and to be clear which "relevant period" is being referred to when using the legislation.

Law: ITA 2007, s. 257AC

13.2.2 Termination date

In practice the termination date relating to relevant shares is the date when all the relief becomes final – i.e., if all the qualifying conditions have been met throughout the period leading up to this date, there is no longer a risk that this might be withdrawn.

Under SEIS, the termination date is specifically referred to as the third anniversary of the share issue date. This contrasts to EIS, where the termination date may be later than the third anniversary if the company has not yet started trading at the time of the share issue.

If an investor makes a disposal of some or all of the shares before the termination date, the relief given will be fully or partially withdrawn, depending on the circumstances.

Law: ITA 2007, s. 257AC(4)

13.2.3 Share issue date

It has been established by case law that the shares are treated as issued once the investor is legally entitled to them. In practice this means when he is entitled to exercise his voting rights, receive dividends, etc. This will be effective once the relevant entries are written into the register of members. Whilst this will often be the same day the shares are paid for and the corresponding certificate is issued to the new shareholders, this is not necessarily always the case.

If there is a delay in making the relevant entries, then the termination date may actually be later than thought. This could be a problem if the shareholder then sells the shares after the third anniversary of paying for them, but before the third anniversary of the entries actually being made in the register. This could prove very costly, so investors should be sure to enquire as to when the entries are made.

Guidance: VCM 33020

13.3 Conditions for the investor

13.3.1 Overview

There are five qualifying conditions that investors must meet to obtain SEIS relief:

1. Neither they nor any associate may be employees of the company in Period B.
2. Neither they nor any associate may have substantial interest in the company in Period A.
3. There must be no related investment arrangements.
4. There must be no linked loans in relation to the investment during Period A.
5. The investment must be made for a genuine commercial purpose, and not as part of tax avoidance scheme.

Law: ITA 2007, s. 257B

13.3.2 Employees

An investor cannot qualify for SEIS income tax relief if he himself, or any associate of his, is an employee of the issuing company, or of any qualifying subsidiary of the issuing company, at any time in Period B – unless the investor or associate was also a director at the same time.

Unlike EIS, company directors are not precluded from claiming relief under SEIS; therefore there is no need for in-depth specific provisions relating to unpaid directors, business angel directors, etc.

As a planning point, the employee restriction only applies in Period B, which starts with the share issue date. It is therefore possible to appoint a potential employee investor as a director before the share issue in order to allow them to claim relief, provided they satisfy the definition of director as given by ITA 2007, s. 257HJ.

Law: ITA 2007, s. 257BA, 257HJ

13.3.3 Substantial interests

An individual will be considered connected to the issuing company if, during Period A, he (alone or together with his associates) directly or indirectly owns or becomes entitled to acquire more than 30% of:

- the ordinary share capital;
- the voting rights; or
- the rights to assets upon a winding up,

in respect of the issuing company.

The presence of the term "indirectly" here prevents an individual from keeping his own interests below the stipulated amounts, whilst concurrently owning additional interests via (say) a company which he controls, or through a trust of which he is the main beneficiary.

In respect of the 30% test, this is not applied in the situation where the initial shareholdings upon incorporation would lead to the threshold being exceeded – i.e. subscriber shares and shareholding ratios are essentially ignored during the period prior to when the company first begins to prepare to carry on the trade.

Example – substantial interest

Bob and Bill form a company together, holding one share each on incorporation. The company does not carry on a trade initially; however, after a month the company issues shares to various SEIS investors, and these funds are used to acquire a trade from another company. Following the new share issues, Bob and Bill own 15% each. Despite the fact that during Period A they owned 50% each, this can be disregarded provided no other changes were made to the share capital prior to the qualifying share issue.

Law: ITA 2007, s. 257BB

13.3.4 Related investment arrangements

No relief can be given under SEIS if an investor has subscribed for shares as part of a reciprocal arrangement. This would be the case, for example, where two investors who owned their own companies colluded together to invest in each other's company to secure relief.

Example – Jack and Jen

Jack and Jen both own 100% of their respective companies Jack Ltd and Jen Ltd. They both need to inject some working capital, some £50,000 each respectively into their companies. Jack and Jen are not related in any way, and are not business partners. They devise a plan together which would see Jack subscribe the £50,000 worth of shares in Jen Ltd and Jen would make a reciprocal investment into Jack Ltd. The idea is that both can claim SEIS relief so that the cost (after relief) would only be half the amount it would otherwise have been. This type of arrangement is caught by the related investment arrangements provision.

Law: ITA 2007, s. 257BC

13.3.5 No linked loans

During Period A, neither the investor nor any of his or her associates must be in receipt of a linked loan. A linked loan is one which in the absence of an investment:

- would not have been made; or
- would not have been made on the same terms.

In most uncomplicated situations (e.g. an outside investor funding a new company), this is unlikely to present a problem when looking directly at the investor-company relationship, because a company seeking to raise capital for a qualifying purpose would not be in a position to be making loans in the first place. The provision is rather intended to catch out schemes or arrangements where the investor essentially gets his money straight back, obtaining a valuable relief with little or no reduction in his or her capital.

This provision does not just apply to loans made from the issuing company (or any of its subsidiaries), however. Any loan that can be linked to the shares issued will fall foul of the rules, where this would not have been made – or would not have been made on the same terms – without the investment taking place.

To illustrate how this might apply in practice, consider the following example:

Example – linked loans

Margaret wants to invest in her friend's new textile manufacturing company. She wishes to invest £100,000 under SEIS, but does not have cash assets. She approaches her bank for a loan, disclosing the purpose in full. The bank agrees to make the loan but insists on taking a charge over the shares in the company as collateral. Because this loan is directly linked to the shares (because of the charge), it is a linked loan, and precludes Margaret from claiming SEIS relief.

In reality a bank is unlikely to accept shares in a company with little or no trading history as collateral; however, the example illustrates the principle.

The meaning of "loan" for these purposes is broadened to include the extension of credit to the investor (or his associates), and the assignment of debts due from the investor (or his associates).

Law: ITA 2007, s. 257BD

13.3.6 Commercial reasoning

In order for an investment to qualify for SEIS relief, it has to be made for a genuine commercial purpose – even if none of the other conditions are breached. The test is subjective, and so is hard to measure or prove; however HMRC guidance does point to certain situations it deems would not be considered commercial. One is where the main motivation for making the investment is benevolence – e.g. putting money into an obviously failing company because of sentimental ties. Another would be an investment made with the sole intention of increasing the share value of another person.

Similarly, there is a general exclusion for investments where the main purpose, or one of the main purposes, of making the investment is the avoidance of tax. It is not thought that simply seeking to access the tax relief itself would constitute avoidance – and so investors do not have to be able to prove that they would have made the investment regardless of the SEIS relief. HMRC have confirmed that, in their opinion, tax avoidance will be a factor in situations where relief has been obtained in circumstances that Parliament did not intend.

Law: ITA 2007, s. 257BE

14. Income tax relief: company conditions

14.1 Overview

In order for a share issue to qualify under SEIS, it must be made by a "qualifying company". Both the legislation and HMRC guidance make frequent reference to this term.

Conditions are set by the legislation ensuring that only smaller, newer, and generally riskier companies are able to access capital via SEIS – as Parliament intended initially. New criteria have recently been introduced to impose further restrictions on the kind of trade a qualifying company can carry out.

Law: ITA 2007, s. 257D

14.2 Conditions to be met by the issuing company

14.2.1 Overview

Section 257D neatly summarises all of the conditions which are pertinent to the issuing company. As mentioned above, the legislation and HMRC guidance make frequent reference to a "qualifying company". The company will only be qualifying if it meets all of the conditions listed in s. 257D, which relate to:

- trading;
- UK permanent establishment;
- financial health;
- unquoted status;
- control and independence;
- no partnerships;
- gross assets;
- number of employees;
- no previous risk capital scheme investments;
- amount raised through SEIS;
- qualifying subsidiaries; and
- property management subsidiaries.

Some of these tests are purely qualitative, and therefore easy to measure – such as the number of employees. Others have a more subjective nature, and therefore judgements must sometimes be exercised, with reliance on case law in some circumstances.

As we saw with the investor, some of the conditions have to be met only at the time of the investment, whereas others must be met for a period of time afterwards as well. Having conditions which are only assessed at the time of investment demonstrates that SEIS is intended to help entrepreneurial businesses grow. It would be counter-productive to the UK economy, for example, to encourage investment in smaller companies, only to remove any incentives to do so if such companies are then successful.

Law: ITA 2007, s. 257D

14.2.2 Trading

The issuing company cannot be a qualifying company unless it exists wholly for the purpose of carrying on one or more new qualifying trades or, alternatively, it is the parent company of a trading group when looking at the group activities as a whole. This condition has to be met throughout Period B. The condition must also have been met for the entirety of the period from incorporation to the start of Period B (i.e. up to the share issue date).

Per VCM 34020, the condition can be viewed as a test of intention, and so the fact that – at the time of the share issue – the trade intended to take place has not yet commenced in the newly formed company should not be fatal to meeting the qualifying company condition. Things may become more complicated if funds held on account are invested into relatively illiquid assets, even if it is intended to realise these for the purposes of commencing trading later on. Simply holding cash on deposit, however, should not pose a problem unless the delay becomes substantial. In practice, HMRC will look at what the directors actually do, rather than what the original stated intention when the company was formed may have been when considering what the company really exists for.

Incidental v substantial

A single company will be considered to be trading if it does not carry on non-qualifying activities other than up to an incidental level. Earning interest on cash held on deposit, therefore, should not preclude such a company from qualifying; however if investment income from various sources forms a substantial part of the company's business turnover it is likely to fail this test. Note that due to the wording of the provision, the non-qualifying activity need not be substantial, merely more than incidental.

If the issuing company is the parent company of a group, it is the activity of the group taken together as a whole that must be considered when looking at non-qualifying activities. This provision is worded slightly differently so that the parent company will only fail the test if the group's non-qualifying activities are substantial. Substantial is taken to mean more than 20%, and should be measured by reference to factors such as turnover, cost overheads, employee and management time commitment, and the employment of assets.

This can lead to a parent company whose group has non-qualifying activities being a qualifying company, where a single company with the same mix of qualifying and non-qualifying activities would fail.

Example – single v group company

A Ltd is a single company which has 85% trading activities, and 15% rental investment activities. B Ltd is the parent company of B group. Its only subsidiary is wholly owned and has exactly the same mix of activities as A Ltd. B Ltd could potentially qualify under SEIS; however A Ltd could not, as 15% is clearly more than incidental.

This could be viewed as an unfair result given that – other than the corporate structure, which is essentially a paper exercise – the underlying activities are identical.

New qualifying trade

A trade is a "new qualifying trade" if it is less than two years old at the investment date, and neither the company nor any qualifying subsidiary has carried on any other trade before the company began to carry on the (new qualifying) trade.

The wording means that a well-established sole trader cannot simply incorporate and issue shares under SEIS, as the whole history of the trade will be taken into account when considering whether it is more than two years old.

In addition, the trade must be conducted on a commercial basis, with a view to realisation of profits, and not consist substantially of carrying on excluded activities.

Qualifying business activity

There is a general condition (discussed in the next chapter) that the money raised through an SEIS investment must be used for the purposes of a qualifying business activity. A qualifying business activity will either constitute a qualifying trade, or preparatory work intended to lead to the commencement of a qualifying trade, either carried out (or intended to be carried out) by the issuing company or by a qualifying 90% subsidiary thereof, provided it is subsequently begun by the relevant entity.

If a company is undertaking research and development intended to lead to the commencement of a qualifying trade, SEIS relief can be granted on issue of the shares; however, preliminary work – such as market research to determine whether the trade is likely to succeed – will not count as research and development for this purpose.

Additionally, there are a number of specified excluded activities which could prevent a company from being a qualifying company, if such activities are substantial. Note that this is slightly different from the test in the section above because some of the specified excluded activities are actually trades themselves. Again, substantial is given to mean 20%.

Broadly, any trade will be qualifying unless it is specifically excluded by the legislation. At the time of writing, the list of excluded activities given by ITA 2007, s. 192 (i.e. the same relevant section for EIS purposes) is as follows:

- Dealing in goods otherwise than in the course of an ordinary trade of wholesale or retail distribution.
- Banking, insurance, money-lending, debt-factoring, hire-purchase financing or other financial activities.
- Leasing (including letting ships on charter or other assets on hire).
- Receiving royalties or licence fees.
- Providing legal or accountancy services.

- Property development.
- Farming or market gardening.
- Holding, managing or occupying woodlands, any other forestry activities or timber production.
- Shipbuilding.
- Producing coal.
- Producing steel.
- Operating or managing hotels or comparable establishments.
- Operating or managing nursing homes or residential care homes.
- Generating or exporting electricity or making electricity generating capacity available.
- Generating heat.
- Generating any form of energy not within the above two points.
- Producing gas or fuel.
- Provision of services or facilities for another business.

Financial activities relate solely to dealing in financial products in one form or another. It is perfectly possible, therefore, for an independent financial adviser to form a limited company and to seek investment by EIS – subject to the usual restrictions regarding insubstantial non-qualifying activities.

Receivership/winding up

It is entirely possible that despite the best endeavours of the directors, the company's business simply fails before the end of Period B. If the trade ceases because the company is placed into administration or receivership, or a petition is made for its winding up, the company will not be treated as having breached the trading conditions, provided the action was taken for genuine commercial reasons. HMRC confirm that if the company ceases the trade because of an expected liquidation, then the sooner the liquidation actually happens following the cessation the more likely it is that relief will not be withdrawn, as it can be established that there will be no return to the investor sooner.

Law: ITA 2007, s. 191, 257DA, 257DB, 257DC, 257HF
Guidance: VCM 34020

14.2.3 UK permanent establishment

A company cannot be a qualifying company for the purposes of SEIS unless it has a permanent establishment in the UK. Section 191A provides that the company will have a UK permanent establishment if one of the following two conditions is met:

- it has a fixed place of business in the UK through which the company's business is wholly or partly carried on; or
- an agent acting on behalf the company has habitually exercised its authority to enter into contracts on behalf of the company.

The most obvious way to qualify is therefore to have a physical presence – i.e. an office building located in the UK from which at least some of the business operates. HMRC guidance at VCM 34050 includes an illustrative list of what they consider to be a fixed place of business:

> "The legislation lists a number of examples, including:
>
> - a place of management;
> - a branch;
> - an office;
> - a factory,
> - a workshop,
> - a mine, oil or gas well,
> - a quarry or any other place of extraction of natural resources; and
> - a building site or construction or installation project.
>
> This list is not intended to be exhaustive; the type of business will determine the type and nature of the premises or facilities required."

If the permanent establishment test cannot be met using the fixed place of business condition, the agent condition can be looked at as an alternative. Here it is key that the agent or agents have authority to enter into contracts as if they were the company itself. A mere employee who would require approval or sign off to enter into a binding contract on behalf the company would be unlikely to meet this condition. The type of contracts the agent is authorised to enter into must also be substantial enough to constitute matters central to the company business, not merely auxiliary services.

In most cases, prospective SEIS qualifying companies will be UK companies anyway; however, it is perfectly possible for a qualifying investment to be made in a non-UK company, provided it has either a fixed place of business or an agent in the UK. Remember, however, that the condition applies to the issuing company, and so an overseas registered parent company will not automatically meet the condition simply because it has a UK subsidiary – it must meet the condition in its own right. The subsidiary itself cannot be the issuing company because of the control and independence requirement (discussed at **14.2.6** below).

Law: ITA 2007, s. 191A, 257DD

14.2.4 Financial health

The company cannot be a qualifying company if, on the date the shares are issued, it is considered to be "in difficulty" as defined by EC guidelines on State aid.

Whether a company is in difficulty for these purposes may be difficult to determine precisely. The guidelines are lengthy; however, a certain amount of common sense and professional opinion should give a feel for the overall health of the company. If there are large losses, high leverage, debts, falling customer numbers, a low or negative balance sheet value, the signs are there that there is at least a question to be asked. That question may be "is this company realistically able to continue operating as a going concern using its own resources, and without outside assistance in the short to medium term?".

HMRC reproduce what they see as the most relevant paragraphs from the EC guidelines at VCM 34060.

The company will not be regarded as being in difficulty if it is newly created – that is to say it is still within its first three years of operations. This is particularly useful for many R&D type companies that are still working to bring a saleable product to market.

Law: ITA 2007, s. 257DE

Guidance:VCM 34060

14.2.5 Unquoted status

This condition is relatively easy to measure. At the time of the investment, the issuing company must be unquoted – that is to say its shares must not be listed on a recognised stock exchange. AIM listed shares are treated as unquoted for these purposes. HMRC guidance also stipulates that some of the PLUS markets were also treated as unquoted; however this is now defunct. PLUS was acquired by ICAP in 2012, and it would appear that its small entrepreneurial markets – e.g. ISDX growth – are also treated as unquoted.

As well as meeting this condition at the time of investment, there must be no existing arrangements for the company to become quoted, or to become a subsidiary of another company which is quoted (or will become quoted as a result of existing arrangements).

Note that these conditions do not prevent the issuing company from becoming successful within Period B and securing a listing due to that success. In that scenario relief would not be withdrawn.

Law: ITA 2007, s. 257DF

14.2.6 Control and independence

At no point during Period A may the issuing company (alone or with any connected persons) control any subsidiaries which are not "qualifying subsidiaries". A qualifying subsidiary is one of which the issuing company directly or indirectly holds more than 50% of the ordinary share capital, and no other person other than the relevant company or its subsidiaries has control of it.

Any "on the shelf" period is ignored for these purposes, so a company purchased directly from a corporate formation company would not fall foul of the test, provided only subscriber shares are in issue, and the company has not begun to carry on, or make preparations for carrying on, any trade or business.

Additionally, the issuing company must be independent during Period A; that is to say it must not itself be under the control of another company – whether alone or with any persons connected to that company. Basically if the issuing company is part of a group, it needs to be the top company.

Law: ITA 2007, s. 257DG

14.2.7 No partnerships

At no time during Period A is the company (or any 90% qualifying subsidiary) permitted to be a member of a partnership. This includes Limited Liability Partnerships, and non-UK entities which are similar in nature to a partnership.

Law: ITA 2007, s. 257DH

14.2.8 Gross assets

Immediately before the share issue, the gross assets of the company (or the aggregated gross assets of a group) must not exceed £200,000. HMRC guidance confirms that any cash received as an advance toward the investment (i.e. conditionally for and in expectation of the share issue) will not be considered to form part of the gross assets.

Law: ITA 2007, s. 257DI

14.2.9 Number of employees

At the time of the investment, the issuing company (or group as a whole) must have fewer than 25 full time equivalent employees (including directors).

Full time for this purpose means an employee who normally works at least 35 hours per week.

Part time employees need to be accounted for, and in doing so their hours need to be aggregated together. For example, two employees who both work 17.5 hours per week together constitute one single full time equivalent for the purpose of the limit.

Only employees who are still working for the company at the issue date need to be accounted for – so seasonal staff may not need to be counted.

Law: ITA 2007, s. 257DJ

14.2.10 No previous risk capital scheme investments

No relief is available if, prior to the investment, the company or any qualifying subsidiary of it has received an investment via EIS or from a VCT . For this reason, it is essential that, where both SEIS and EIS issues are intended to take place, the SEIS issue happens first.

The requirement to have spent at least 70% of moneys raised via SEIS before an investment under EIS can take place was removed with effect from 6 April 2015.

It is often the case that investors will seek relief under both SEIS and EIS for what is materially one investment. This is permissible provided the SEIS investment takes place first. The tribunal cases of *X-Wind Power Limited* and *GDR Food Technology Limited* have established that relief under SEIS will be lost where the EIS1 form is submitted instead of the SEIS1 form in these cases. Unfortunately, once a compliance statement under EIS is issued, it can no longer be said that the condition for no previous risk capital scheme investments to have been made is met.

Law: ITA 2007, s. 257DK

Cases: *X-Wind Power Limited v HMRC* [2016] UKFTT 317 (TC); *GDR Food Technology Limited v HMRC* [2016] UKFTT 466 (TC)

14.2.11 Maximum amount raised

The investments through SEIS (and any other *de minimis* State aid) in the three year rolling period, ending with the date of the relevant share issue, cannot exceed £150,000. If a particular investment leads to this limit being breached; only the portion that does not exceed the £150,000 limit attracts any relief. An investor would therefore have a mix of qualifying and non-qualifying shares, and this would need to be considered if relief needed to be reduced later on.

Law: ITA 2007, s. 257DL

14.2.12 Qualifying subsidiaries

There is a specific condition that if the issuing company has any subsidiaries during Period B, they must be qualifying subsidiaries as discussed above.

Law: ITA 2007, s. 191, 257DM, 257HJ

14.2.13 Property management subsidiaries

An extension to the general condition regarding qualifying subsidiaries is that if any of the company's subsidiaries carries on a business which is mainly that of holding land or property deriving value from land, that subsidiary has to be a 90% subsidiary (rather than just a 51% subsidiary).

Of course the overall impact of the non-qualifying activity would also need to be reviewed to determine whether it is "substantial".

Law: ITA 2007, s. 257DN

15. Income tax relief: general requirements

15.1 Introduction

In addition to the specific requirements to be met by the investor and the issuing company, there are a number of conditions which are grouped together in the legislation under the heading "general requirements". These conditions relate to the nature of the investment itself.

It is worth noting at the outset that the issuing company itself has to carry on the qualifying trade, unless the activities are carried out by a qualifying 90% subsidiary. There is, however, no requirement that a 90% subsidiary needs to be UK resident, and so shares could be issued by a UK parent company with the funds raised diverted entirely offshore.

15.2 General requirements

15.2.1 Overview

The conditions set out by the legislation are those related to:

- the shares;
- purpose of the issue;
- use of the money;
- pre-arranged exits;
- tax avoidance; and
- disqualifying arrangements.

We will consider each of these in turn.

Law: ITA 2007, s. 257C

15.2.2 Shares

In order to qualify for SEIS relief, the shares issued must form part of the ordinary share capital of the company, with no present or future preferential rights in respect of dividends, redemption, or to the company's assets upon a winding up, for the entirety of Period B. The purpose of this restriction is to ensure that investors are participating in the company on a full risk basis.

The shares must be subscribed for in cash, and fully paid up at the time they are issued to the investor. Any delay between the share issue and the funds being received could see relief being denied. Second hand shares do not qualify for relief under SEIS.

It is often the case in practice that SEIS shares are issued under a separate class – e.g. B shares. The restriction does not prevent separate dividends being voted to the holders of the SEIS shares in this case, provided the shares carry the same different rights to dividends as other classes of shares. In practice, however, it is unlikely that dividends will be paid on SEIS shares – at least in early years.

Ordinary share capital is defined by ITA 2007, s. 989 such that it:

> "... in relation to a company, means all the company's issued share capital (however described), other than the capital the holders of which have a right to a dividend at a fixed rate, but have no other right to share in the company's profits."

Per HMRC guidance:

> "A right carried by a share is a preferential right if that right takes priority over a right carried by some other share. Thus where a company has only one class of issued share capital no share carries any preferential right.
>
> The rights carried by ordinary shares may in some cases be preferential as compared with the rights of deferred shares, but this is not necessarily so. In particular, where deferred shares carry a purely theoretical right to a residue of assets in a winding up (for example where, in the case of a very small company, after the first £20million has been distributed to ordinary shareholders the deferred shareholders are entitled to 1p per share) we do not regard the ordinary shares as carrying a preferential right.
>
> Where a company has two classes of issued share capital, and dividends are declared on one class but not on the other, the right of the former class is not a preferential right."

Law: ITA 2007, s. 257CA, 989

Guidance: VCM 33020

15.2.3 Purpose of the issue

The shares must be issued in order to raise money to fund a qualifying activity carried on, or to be carried on, by the issuing company or a qualifying 90% subsidiary. A number of cases which considered EIS relief in this context (e.g. *Optos, Forthright (Wales) Ltd*) are applicable to SEIS, as the provision is virtually identical to its EIS counterpart.

Law: ITA 2007, s. 257CB

Cases: *Forthright (Wales) Ltd v Davies* (2004) 76 TC 138; *Optos plc v R&C Commrs* (2006) Sp C 560

15.2.4 Spending of money raised

The money raised by the share issue has to be spent for a qualifying purpose by the end of Period B.

Relief will not be lost if an amount of the money raised which is not significant is not so employed. Exactly what constitutes "significant" for these purposes is unclear, and will probably need to be reviewed in light of the total amount raised.

Note that the requirement for the money to be "spent", compared with "employed" under EIS provisions, means that measuring the condition is far more simple - the money raised must be extinguished; there is no concept of specifically earmarked funds avoiding a breach of the condition.

Law: ITA 2007, s. 257CC, 257HG

15.2.5 Pre-arranged exits

Relief will be denied on any shares issued under arrangements which would effectively guarantee (or at least make it likely) that the investor will receive his or her money back at some point in the future through some mechanism.

Arrangements caught by this provision are set out in s. 257CD:

> "(a) arrangements with a view to the subsequent repurchase, exchange or other disposal of those shares or of other shares in or securities of the issuing company,

(b) arrangements for or with a view to the cessation of any trade which is being or is to be or may be carried on by the issuing company or a person connected with that company,

(c) arrangements for the disposal of, or of a substantial amount (in terms of value) of, the assets of the issuing company or of a person connected with that company, or

(d) arrangements the main purpose or one of the main purposes of which is (by means of any insurance, indemnity or guarantee or otherwise) to provide partial or complete protection for persons investing in shares in the issuing company against what would otherwise be the risks attached to making the investment."

The most straightforward arrangements which might be seen (or at least suggested) in practice would be a guaranteed undertaking on behalf of the company to repurchase the shares at purchase price after the termination date provided a success hurdle is met. The idea is that the investor then gets back the cash used to make the investment whilst banking the tax relief. This would be sufficient to disqualify the investment from SEIS.

HMRC do make clear that there is nothing wrong with a company indicating to potential investors how they feel that the value in the shares may be realised at some later date – as, of course, genuine investors will be seeking to make a return on the investment.

Law: ITA 2007, s. 257CD

15.2.6 No tax avoidance

As with most government endorsed tax reliefs, relief cannot be given unless the transaction is entered into for a genuine commercial purpose and not as part of a scheme or arrangement, the main purpose (or one of the main purposes) of which is the avoidance of tax.

HMRC confirm that simply making an investment with the aim of it qualifying for SEIS relief (as opposed to one which clearly would not), and receiving the associated tax reduction, is clearly not in and of itself tax avoidance.

Law: ITA 2007, s. 257CE

15.2.7 Disqualifying arrangements

The concept of disqualifying arrangements was introduced in April 2012 – at the same time as SEIS took effect. If the shares are issued under arrangements which are "disqualifying", no relief can be attributed to them.

Arrangements will be disqualifying if either condition A or B is met.

Condition A is that as a result (direct or indirect) of the money raised by the share issue, all or most of that money (or an equivalent amount) is subsequently paid to or for the benefit of a relevant person or persons.

A relevant person is one who is party to the arrangements, or someone connected to such a person.

Example

Bill invests £100,000 in Mark's company, A Ltd. Shortly afterwards, A Ltd spends £90,000 on marketing services provided by B Ltd – a company wholly owned by Bill's wife. This would appear to fall foul of the disqualifying arrangement provision under Condition A for SEIS purposes.

Condition B is applicable in circumstances where, in the absence of the arrangements, it would have been reasonable to expect that the whole or greater part of the component activities of the relevant business activity would have been carried on as part of another business by a person or by persons who are party to the arrangements or a person or persons connected with such a party.

This appears to prevent situations where an otherwise non-qualifying entity wishes to start a new venture, and does so through a newly formed company owned and run by others, for the sole reason that SEIS relief would not otherwise be available.

HMRC's guidance indicates that the purpose of the arrangements in question will be scrutinised to determine whether they create an activity, or an appearance of one, with the result that relief would be available (but for the "disqualifying" provision).

"Examples might include (without necessarily being limited to):

- cases where a business appears to be fragmented in a way which is commercially unusual with the result that there is a company which (apart from this test) meets the qualifying conditions for the schemes;
- cases where a transaction which would normally be expected to be between two parties, involves three (or more) parties, where the additional party is a company which (apart from this test) meets the qualifying conditions for the schemes;
- cases where the economic substance of a company's activity appears to be at odds with its form (for instance, where contractual arrangements appear designed to generate an outcome similar to a lending or credit facility whilst the contracts are not immediately obviously loan or credit contracts in legal form)."

Overall the provision is intended to prevent promoters offering SEIS type products as an off the shelf solution for those seeking to avoid or mitigate tax with no real interest in entrepreneurial investment.

Where disqualifying arrangements are suspected by HMRC, the Small Companies Enterprise Centre (SCEC) may not be willing to issue an advance assurance opinion, meaning that the likelihood of a successful application for a compliance statement is less certain. The only option if this is the case is to go ahead with the share issue, and apply via form SEIS1. This can present a problem because the investors will often refuse to invest in the absence of an advance assurance opinion, as it gives the impression that HMRC view the company negatively in respect of SEIS relief.

Of course it is worth remembering that an advance assurance opinion is not a guarantee of a subsequent application leading to a compliance statement being issued; though this is unlikely to appease investors who place reliance upon the assurance.

It might be possible to avoid employing any of the funds until after the application for the compliance statement has been made, and answer received. In the event of the application being unsuccessful the company could then always offer to repurchase the shares from the investors; however it could not be compelled to do so, or it would risk falling foul of the pre-arranged exits provisions discussed earlier (see **15.2.5**).

In any event, the use of such an arrangement would appear to be contrary to the intentions of SEIS generally.

Law: ITA 2007, s. 257CF

15.2.8 Risk to capital requirement

Finance Act 2018 contains a new condition for investments to ensure that investments are made at full risk to the investor's capital. The new provision is included as s. 257AAA.

Over the years, a number of schemes have been marketed that purport to take advantage of SEIS relief, but are aimed at "capital preservation". This could be achieved by investment in a company, or portfolio of companies, where there is little chance of capital movement, either up or down. The idea is that after the termination date, the company buys back the shares at subscription price, and the investor has banked the 50% income tax relief.

From the point of view of the company, it is arguable that the investment constitutes an interest-free loan; however, in practice companies affiliated with a capital preservation scheme are likely to have been set up specifically to receive the investment and just about meet the requirements for relief to be given, undertaking a low-risk trade.

This is especially powerful if combined with inheritance tax planning, as SEIS shares will generally qualify for business property relief after two years, and so there is a clear incentive for sheltering what would otherwise be taxable cash in this way, as the shares could be sold by the beneficiaries of the will.

Unsurprisingly, HMRC do not view these arrangements as genuine investments in the spirit of the SEIS framework. Whilst the "no tax avoidance" requirement might catch them out, the new condition is more explicit.

For investments made on or after 15 March 2018 (the date specified in the original tax policy note), relief will only be given if, at the time of the investment, it is reasonable to conclude that both:

- the investee company has an objective to grow and develop its trade in the long term; and
- there is a significant risk that the investor could lose more of the capital invested than he or she gets back by way of other returns from the investment.

The second condition means that investments that have little or no probability of anything but small movements in value – say plus or minus 10% – might not qualify as this is far lower than the 50% income tax relief.

The condition will be assessed giving due consideration and regard to any circumstances existing at the time of the investment. The new s. 257AAA (3) sets out a non-exhaustive list of circumstances that will be considered:

(a) the extent to which the company's objectives include increasing the number of its employees or the turnover of its trade;

(b) the nature of the company's sources of income, including the extent to which there is a significant risk of the company not receiving some or all of the income;

(c) the extent to which the company has or is likely to have assets, or is or could become a party to arrangements for acquiring assets, that could be used to secure financing from any person;

(d) the extent to which the activities of the company are subcontracted to persons who are not connected with it;

(e) the nature of the company's ownership structure or management structure, including the extent to which others participate in or devise the structure;

(f) how any opportunity for investment in the company is marketed; and

(g) the extent to which arrangements are in place under which opportunities for investments in the company are or may be marketed with, or otherwise associated with, opportunities for investments in other companies or entities.

Law: ITA 2007, s. 257AAA

16. Income tax relief: withdrawal of relief

16.1 Overview

The preceding chapters mainly considered conditions which would preclude SEIS relief from being granted on application. We will now consider situations where relief is initially granted, but has to be withdrawn due to a disqualifying event before the termination date.

In some cases, relief is only partially withdrawn, and a calculation is necessary to determine how much. This will consequently affect any loss relief claimed on the shares (if applicable), as the allowable loss is adjusted for any income tax relief given which has not yet been withdrawn. We will consider this in further detail later on.

It should be noted at the outset that HMRC have the power to raise a discovery assessment under TMA 1970, s. 29 if they discover that any of the information on the SEIS1 form was incorrect.

Law: TMA 1970, s. 29; ITA 2007, s. 257F

16.2 Changes of circumstances before termination date

As alluded to in the preceding chapters, a number of the specific conditions have to be met right up to the termination date of the relevant shares, not just at the date of the share issue. These conditions have been discussed in detail already.

16.3 Disposals

16.3.1 Introduction

In addition to breaching the ongoing qualifying conditions discussed at **16.2** above, relief will be wholly or partly withdrawn in most circumstances where the investor makes a disposal of the shares before the end of Period B. This is the third anniversary of the share issue date.

For this reason it is essential to determine exactly when the share issue date is. This is discussed at **13.2.3** above.

Relief is not withdrawn if the shares are transferred to a spouse or civil partner who is living with the investor at the time of the transfer.

Law: ITA 2007, s. 257FA

16.3.2 Disposal not at arm's length

If a disposal takes place before the end of Period B, and does not take place on arm's-length terms, the SEIS relief will be withdrawn in full.

A bargain is generally held to be made at arm's-length if all parties to the transaction have acted in such a way as to get the best deal for themselves. The fact that an individual may not have got the best terms possible does not necessarily mean that the bargain was not made on arm's-length terms – the crucial factor is the intention. A bargain cannot be said to be made on arm's-length terms if there is an intention by one party to confer a gratuitous benefit on another. This would include a situation where a shareholder knowingly sells his shares for much less than they are worth.

Note that (contrary to popular misconception), a disposal may be held to have taken place otherwise than on arm's-length terms even if the parties are unconnected.

Law: ITA 2007, s. 257FA(2)

16.3.3 Disposal at arm's length

Where an early disposal does take place on arm's-length terms, relief is only fully withdrawn if the sales proceeds are equal to or greater than the subscription price. Where the sales proceeds (if any) do not exceed the subscription price, a partial withdrawal of relief takes place. The amount of relief withdrawn is calculated using the following formula:

> Relief withdrawn = sales proceeds x original SEIS rate of relief

Example – Maggie

Maggie subscribed for 1,000 shares in SEIS Ltd for £100,000 on 31 December 2017, claiming SEIS income tax relief of £50,000. Maggie sold all her shares for £40,000 on 1 June 2019. This is before the termination date, being before the third anniversary of the investment.

The relief withdrawn will be 50% x £40,000 = £20,000. The remaining £30,000 is not withdrawn.

Where a partial withdrawal is made, the calculation for an allowable loss is affected as this depends on relief which was given but not withdrawn.

The partial withdrawal provisions protect investors who have made genuine commercial investments, but who can clearly see that the company has not been successful. They can therefore cut their losses and receive at least some proceeds for the shares without being penalised by a full withdrawal of the relief.

Law: ITA 2007, s. 257FA(3)

16.3.4 Part disposals

SEIS relief given in respect of a particular share issue is treated as accruing evenly across all shares acquired. If, therefore, only part of the holding is sold prior to the termination date, only a proportion of the relief is withdrawn accordingly.

If the shares are sold for a marginal profit, the apportionment is fairly straightforward. So if 40% of the shares held are disposed of before the termination date, 40% of the original relief will be withdrawn. The situation is slightly more complicated where the shares are sold at a loss.

Example – Maggie (continued) – part disposal

Consider Maggie's situation from above again; however this time she only disposes of 600 shares for £25,000. Because the relief is deemed to accrue evenly over the subscription, these 600 shares account for £30,000 of the original relief.

The amount to be withdrawn will be £25,000 x 50% = £12,500. The remaining 400 shares account for £20,000 of SEIS relief, and any further withdrawal cannot exceed this £20,000 – even if the shares are sold before the termination date at a profit. The relief not withdrawn on disposal of the 600 shares (i.e. £17,500) is never withdrawn.

One further consideration needed is the situation where full relief could not be utilised, for example where there was not sufficient income tax liability to use the maximum relief. In the circumstances, the calculation for the reduction is amended as follows:

> Relief withdrawn = sales proceeds x original rate of relief x A/B

where:

> A = the actual tax reduction given in £s
>
> B = the maximum possible tax reduction (i.e. qualifying investment x SEIS rate).

Law: ITA 2007, s. 257FA

16.3.5 Acquisition of issuing company

In most circumstances, the takeover of the issuing company by another company will lead to SEIS relief being withdrawn because of the requirement for it to be independent throughout Period B. If all the shares are sold for cash then all of the relief will be withdrawn, even if the sale is technically for a loss. This is because ceasing to meet the independence requirement would mean that the company is no longer a qualifying company.

In contrast, if a reorganisation involves the insertion of a brand new parent company above the issuing company, and the investors receive shares in the parent company in exchange for their own, relief may not necessarily be withdrawn. The circumstances where this applies are set out in s. 257HB. Broadly, clearance must have been given that HMRC are satisfied that the exchange has been made for genuine commercial reasons before this section can apply. The consideration for the old shares must consist solely of shares in the new parent company, and the acquiring company must acquire all of the shares in the issuing company.

One particular requirement is that the acquiring company is only permitted to have subscriber shares in issue. This means that following incorporation, no further shares are permitted to have been issued. To illustrate, consider a parent company founded by four shareholders holding a single share each. Section 257HB can apply if this company, unchanged, takes over an issuing company by means of the qualifying share for share exchange. Conversely, if following the original founding of the company, some further shares are issued then s. 257HB cannot apply. This (and the meaning of subscriber shares) was confirmed in the EIS case of *Finn* where a reverse takeover method was adopted.

Law: ITA 2007, s. 257HB

Case: *Finn and Others v HMRC* [2015] UKFTT 144 (TC)

16.3.6 Share identification

In some circumstances it may transpire that an investor holds a mix of shares in the issuing company acquired on the same day or different days, and/or that attracted either income tax relief, SEIS reinvestment relief, both, or neither depending on the particular prevailing conditions at the time the respective share issues took place. If this is the case then the shares disposed of must be carefully identified in accordance with the special identification rules set out in s. 257HA.

The identification rules are relatively easy to follow, and essentially provide that the shares are not pooled as normally, but are treated as being disposed on a first-in first-out basis. In circumstances where shares attracting different relief are acquired on the same day, the rules stipulate that shares to which no relief is attached are treated as being disposed of first, followed by shares only attracting income tax relief (but not reinvestment relief), and finally shares attracting both.

Additionally, where some of the shares have been subject to a carry back claim, those shares are treated as being disposed of before others acquired on the same day.

Law: ITA 2007, s. 257HA

16.4 Options

If the relevant shares become subject to either a put or call option at any time before the termination date, this will also be treated as a disposal and all relief will be withdrawn.

A call option is one which would bind the investor to sell the shares to the option holder, or other nominated person. In practice, this could only occur after the investor acquires the shares.

A put option is one which would bind the grantor of the option to purchase the shares.

Law: ITA 2007, s. 257FC, 257FD

16.5 Value received

16.5.1 Overview

SEIS relief will be wholly or partially withdrawn if the investor receives value from the issuing company at any time during Period A. Recall that this begins with the incorporation of the company, and ends immediately before the termination date (see **13.2.1**). No withdrawal is necessary if the receipt is insignificant, or the value is subsequently replaced (see below).

The rule is extended to receipts that come from persons connected to the issuing company as well as just the company itself, and to situations where the recipient of the value is an associate of the investor.

Law: ITA 2007, s. 257FE

16.5.2 When is value received?

The occasions when value is considered as received for these purposes are set out by s. 257FH. Broadly, any payment made in respect of the relevant shares invested in – i.e. related to those shares – will be caught, other than certain exceptions which are set out accordingly in the section.

Example – value received

John invests in A Ltd via SEIS during 2018. Shortly after the investment, the company repays a debt of £40,000 in respect of genuine services provided to the company by John. The credit is three months old, which is considered normal compared to other customers John has. This payment is not value received because it is discharged as an ordinary trade debt as per s. 257FH(13)(a).

Section 257FI then sets out how to measure the amount of value received in each circumstance. HMRC guidance at VCM 36070 contains a handy table combining the instances where value is received, with the measurement of that value. The table (reproduced below) is useful, but is no substitute for familiarity with the contents of s. 257FI.

HMRC table reproduced from VCM 36070		
1	The company repays, redeems or repurchases any of its share capital or securities belonging to the individual.	The amount receivable or, if greater, the market value of the shares or securities.
2	The company makes a payment to the individual for giving up his right to any of its the shares or securities on their cancellation or extinguishment.	The amount receivable or, if greater, the market value of shares or securities market.
3	The company repays a debt owed to the individual. A debt incurred after the issue of the relevant shares is not taken into account for this, unless that debt replaced an earlier debt incurred before the share issue.	The amount receivable or, if greater, the value of the debt.
4	The company makes a payment to the individual for giving up his right to any debt on its extinguishment. ('ordinary trade debts' and debts in respect of payments listed at VCM36070 are excepted from this rule).	The amount receivable or, if greater, the market value of the debt.
5	The company releases or waives any liability of the individual to the company. In addition to an actual release or waiver, a company is treated as having released or waived liability if the individual fails to discharge a liability owed to the company within 12 months of the time when it ought have been discharged.	The amount of the liability.
6	The company discharges, or undertakes to discharge, an individual's liability to a third person.	The amount of the liability.
7	The company makes a loan or advance to the individual other than one repaid in full before the issue of the shares.	The amount of the loan or advance.

HMRC table reproduced from VCM 36070		
8	The company provides a benefit or facility for the individual.	The cost to the company of providing the benefit facility less a consideration given for it by the individual.
9	The company transfers an asset to the individual for no consideration or consideration less than its market value.	The difference between the market value of the asset and any consideration given for it.
10	The individual transfers an asset to the company for a consideration in excess of its market value.	The difference between the market value of the asset and the consideration received for it.
11	The company makes any other payment to the individual, except payments within VCM36060 or one made in discharge of an 'ordinary trade debt' – see below.	The amount of the payment.
12	The individual receives any payment or asset in connection with the winding up or dissolution of the company.	The amount of the payment or market value of the asset.
13	The individual disposes of any share capital or securities, or rights over such shares to: • A person who has a 'substantial interest' in the company • Any employee of the company • Any director of the company	The amount receivable or, if greater, the market value of the shares.

An excluded payment is one which is paid to a director or shareholder where the payment is one which is reasonable to expect a director and/or shareholder to receive in the course of their services in the respective positions. Ordinary dividends, commercial interest on loans, and reimbursements of reasonable expenses are therefore excluded payments. Reasonable remuneration is also excluded provided that it is in exchange for services provided in the course of a trade or profession (apart from secretarial or managerial services – or services the issuing company itself provides), where the profits of that trade or profession (including the remuneration) will be chargeable to income tax.

Section 257FH(2) also provides that reasonable remuneration paid for the director's services (including any benefit made available) whilst acting in that capacity is not treated as value received. Where the individual is an employee as well as a director, any payments made in respect of the employment are treated as payments made in respect of the directorship for the purposes of this section – i.e. they are not treated as value received unless they are unreasonable.

Law: ITA 2007, s. 257FH

Guidance: VCM 36070

16.5.3 Withdrawal amount

The calculation to determine how much SEIS relief must be withdrawn is virtually identical to that for a premature disposal (see **16.3.3** above). In the case of value received, however, the amount of the value replaces the sales proceeds in the formula. The provision for circumstances where SEIS relief was not able to be claimed in full due to insufficient income is also the same.

Where value is received, and it will affect two or more share investments (i.e. Period A has not yet elapsed), the reduction is applied proportionately to each group of shares by reference to the SEIS relief that was obtained on each investment relative to the total relief given on all relevant share issues. Similarly, where some of the relief was given in the tax year prior to the investment following an election to carry back, the reduction is split proportionately in the same way.

Law: ITA 2007, s. 257FE(2)

16.5.4 Insignificant receipts

Value received will be ignored if it is insignificant. Insignificant means either:

- less than £1,000; or
- if more than £1,000, insignificant compared to the amount subscribed by the individual for the relevant shares.

If reliance is to be sought on the second point, then a subjective test will need to be carried out and agreement reached with HMRC.

Where there are multiple receipts in Period A which individually would be "insignificant", they must be aggregated and considered collectively.

Law: ITA 2007, s. 257FF

16.6 Replacement value

Where value has been received, there is scope for the investor to return the value to the person that it was received from. This is referred to as replacement value. If the value was received by an associate, it is the associate who must return the value rather than the individual. Similarly, if the payment was made not by the SEIS company but by a connected person, the return of value must go to that person.

When making a payment of replacement value, the way that value was received should be mirrored – i.e. if the value was the transfer of an asset at undervalue, an asset should be transferred back at a corresponding over value. If the value received was a cash payment, the repayment should be in cash, which is not one of the following:

- a reasonable payment for goods, services or facilities;
- a payment of interest on normal commercial terms;
- a payment of a dividend which does not exceed a normal return on the investment;
- a payment for an asset not exceeding its market value;
- a payment of rent on normal commercial terms; or
- a payment to discharge a trade debt.

In order for the provision to apply, the amount received must be returned in full – there is no credit given for a part return. The value must be replaced without unreasonable delay. In practice this means as soon as is reasonably possible following the discovery of the value receipt.

If the value received has been the subject of an appeals process, it needs to be replaced within 60 days of the final determination.

Where it is accepted that the value has been replaced, there will accordingly be no withdrawal or reduction of relief.

Law: ITA 2007, s. 257FN

16.7 Acquisition of trade or share capital

There are two provisions which aim to restrict SEIS relief to genuine outside investors. These provisions prevent the issuing company from acquiring a trade previously carried on by the owners of the issuing company, or the share capital of a company which carried on the trade which the investor controlled.

Section 257FP acts to withdraw any relief given to an individual if a trade (or the majority of the assets used to carry out a trade) is acquired by the issuing company during Period A, and at any time, the individual (alone or together with another group of individuals):

- owned more than a half share in the trade (unincorporated businesses) during Period A; or
- controlled the company that previously carried on the trade (where the trade is carried on by a company) at any time.

As is often the case, the interests of any associated persons are aggregated with those of the individual for these purposes.

Note that the trade does not have to be acquired directly from the individual for the relief to be withdrawn.

Example – trade acquisition

Ben is a sole trader until he sells the trade to his friend Bill on 5 April 2018. On 31 December 2018, Ben invests in SEIS Ltd claiming relief under SEIS. Two years later SEIS Ltd acquires the trade from Bill for genuine reasons. Because Ben owned the trade previously, the SEIS relief has to be withdrawn.

Section 257FQ is essentially an identical provision, covering the situation where the shares of a company that carried on the trade are purchased by the issuing company instead of the trade and assets.

Law: ITA 2007, s. 257FP, 257FQ

16.8 Relief subsequently found not to have been due

It is the responsibility of the investor or issuing company to notify HMRC in circumstances where their respective qualifying conditions are not met throughout the relevant time period. For example, the investor must notify HMRC if the relief needs to be withdrawn because he is no longer a qualifying investor, and the company must notify HMRC if it breaches the maximum permitted amount raised under risk finance investments during Period B.

HMRC have wide ranging powers to request information from investors, the issuing company, persons connected with it, or parties to any arrangements related to the share issue.

Section 257FR gives HMRC the power to withdraw relief where the company does not give notice, and, in an officer's opinion:

- the company is not a qualifying company; or
- the shares were not issued to raise money for the purpose of a qualifying business activity; or
- the company using the money raised does not satisfy the conditions applying to it, or
- the money raised was not employed for the purpose of a qualifying business activity within the time allowed.

The officer must give notice to the issuing company (not the investor), stating the reason he intends to withdraw the relief. The company has the right to appeal the decision; however, the officer is entitled to raise assessments on the individual investors before the appeal is heard. This may be done to protect any assessment from falling out of time, though normally collection will not be sought before the appeal is heard.

Law: ITA 2007, s. 257FR

17. CGT reinvestment relief

17.1 The relief

17.1.1 Overview

SEIS reinvestment relief is similar to the EIS deferral relief in terms of its operation. However, rather than simply postponing payment of the tax on a gain matched to a qualifying investment, reinvestment relief exempts part of the otherwise chargeable gain where the proceeds are reinvested in qualifying shares. Provided the shares qualify for SEIS relief, and are held until the end of Period A, that part of the gain is never subject to CGT. The investor has to claim, and obtain, SEIS income tax relief on the shares used for the reinvestment, and so the reinvestment itself may be exempt from CGT upon a later disposal (see **Chapter 18**).

The relief works by reducing the amount of the gain matched with a qualifying SEIS share investment by the relevant percentage. The relevant percentage is 100% for the tax year ended 5 April 2013, and 50% for all subsequent tax years.

Note that where the relevant percentage is 50%, the remaining 50% of the gain remains chargeable; there is no scope under SEIS to defer this remainder. However, in practice an investment under SEIS takes place alongside an investment under EIS, and so the remainder can be deferred using the EIS deferral provisions in these circumstances.

Unlike EIS deferral relief, the amount that can be matched via a qualifying investment is capped at the annual permitted maximum amount for SEIS income tax relief – currently £100,000.

Law: TCGA 1992, Sch. 5BB

17.1.2 Reinvestment window

In order to be capable of being matched to a SEIS investment, the gains must arise within a four year time window, commencing three years before, and ending one year after, the share issue date.

An alternative way of thinking about this is that once the taxpayer realises any capital gains, he has three years to make an SEIS investment and defer some or all of them, or he can match them to an SEIS investment made within the preceding 12 months.

A gain arising prior to 6 April 2012 cannot be matched to an SEIS investment for the purposes of reinvestment relief, because SEIS did not exist before that date. Practitioners should be aware of this in the event that they are advising on reinvestment relief claims relating to earlier years. The time limit for making a claim is five years from 31 January following the end of the tax year in which the shares either were issued, or were treated as issued in the event of carry-back claim.

Law: TCGA 1992, Sch. 5BB, para. 3

17.1.3 Operation of the relief

The relief works by reducing eligible gains by up to 50% of the amount of the qualifying investment in the SEIS company; however this is restricted and cannot exceed:

- the amount of SEIS expenditure specified in the claim;
- the amount of SEIS expenditure that is unused, or
- the part of the gain that is unmatched.

The effect of this is that no more than 50% of a gain can be offset by SEIS reinvestment relief, even if 50% of the qualifying SEIS investment is more than that amount.

Example – reinvestment restricted

Siân makes a taxable gain of £80,000 during 2017-18. On 6 April 2018, she makes a qualifying SEIS investment of £100,000 for 500,000 shares. She can reduce her taxable gain by £40,000.

The reinvestment relief is apportioned equally across all shares to which the claim is applicable – so in Siân's case, each SEIS share carries £40,000/500,000 = 8p of the exempt gain. This is important to note if relief has to be partly withdrawn later on – for example in the case of a part disposal prior to the termination date.

Law: TCGA 1992, Sch. 5BB, para. 1

17.2 Restrictions

Reinvestment relief is restricted if:

- income tax relief is not attributable on some of the shares invested in; or
- income tax relief has been withdrawn or reduced.

Law: TCGA 1992, Sch. 5BB, para. 2

17.2.1 Income tax relief not obtained in full

If the investor breaches the annual permitted maximum investment amount of £100,000, only part of the shareholding will qualify for SEIS income tax relief. This was discussed at **14.2.11**.

Where this is the case, the amount of SEIS expenditure that can be included in the reinvestment claim is restricted to the qualifying proportion.

Example – restriction

Amy subscribes for £150,000 of shares in SEIS Ltd in 2018-19, and wishes to match this expenditure to a gain of £170,000 arising in the same year. The amount of expenditure which can be so matched is restricted to £100,000. After reinvestment relief, being 50% of this amount, the gain is reduced to £120,000.

Where there are two or more subscriptions in a tax year which exceed the total when aggregated together, the qualifying expenditure is attributed proportionally to each subscription by reference to the amount of the respective investments, i.e.:

$$\frac{\text{SEIS expenditure in company}}{\text{Total expenditure on SEIS shares in tax year}} \times £100{,}000$$

HMRC guidance at VCM 45060 uses an example to illustrate this in practice.

HMRC example

In 2012-13 an individual investor carries out the following transactions.

- He disposes of a property under an unconditional contract dated 1 May 2012 giving rise to an agreed chargeable gain of £130,000.
- He subscribes £40,000 for, and is issued with shares in, a SEIS company A Ltd on 1 September 2012.
- He subscribes £120,000 for, and is issued with further shares in, another SEIS company B Ltd on 1 December 2012.

He claims full SEIS Income Tax Relief in respect both share issues. He also makes claims for re-investment relief in respect of the amounts subscribed for the shares in both A Ltd and B Ltd.

Section 257AB(2)(b) ITA07 limits the amount on which the investor's SEIS Income Tax relief is based to £100,000.

Of the £40,000 subscribed for the shares in A Ltd the amount that can be matched with the chargeable gain is limited to

$$\frac{£40{,}000}{£160{,}000} \text{x } £100{,}000 = £25{,}000$$

Of the £120,000 subscribed for the shares in B Ltd the amount that can be matched with the chargeable gain is limited to

$$\frac{£120{,}000}{£160{,}000} \text{x } £100{,}000 = £75{,}000$$

The chargeable gain on the property is reduced to £30,000.

Had the transactions been carried out instead in 2013-14, the amounts subscribed for shares that could be matched with the chargeable gain would again be limited to a total of £100,000. After re-investment relief of £50,000 (see VCM45020) the gain on the property would be reduced to £80,000.

Law: ITA 2007, s. 257AB; TCGA 1992, Sch. 5BB, para. 2

Guidance: VCM 45060

17.2.2 Income tax relief reduced

Income tax relief is withdrawn or reduced where value is received in Period A, or if qualifying shares are disposed of (or treated as disposed of) prior to the termination date.

In the case of value received, this can occur prior to a claim for reinvestment relief being made (or even prior to the share issue). Where this is the case, the amount of available expenditure should be adjusted when calculating and claiming the reinvestment relief. There is therefore no need for a withdrawal of the exemption, which will be the case if the reduction in income tax happens *after* the reinvestment relief has been claimed.

Law: TCGA 1992, Sch. 5BB, para. 2

17.3 Withdrawal of relief

If income tax relief has to be withdrawn or reduced because of events discussed in **Chapter 16**, there will also be a withdrawal or reduction of the reinvestment relief. If income tax relief is fully withdrawn – because, for example, the shares are disposed of in Period B for a non-arm's length bargain – reinvestment relief is also withdrawn in full. The entire gain not originally charged to CGT is then treated as accruing in the year of the share issue (rather than the year in which the event triggering the reduction took place).

Where relief is reduced, for example where some of the shares are disposed of, or where value not exceeding the qualifying investment amount is received, the reinvestment relief is reduced in the same proportion as the income tax relief. This is calculated using the formula:

$$\text{Reduction in reinvestment relief} = \text{original reinvestment relief x } \frac{R1 - R2}{R1}$$

where:

R1 = the SEIS income tax relief prior to applying the reduction; and

R2 = SEIS income tax relief following the reduction.

Example – reduction

Maisy subscribed for 100,000 shares costing £100,000 in 2017-18, claiming SEIS income tax relief of £50,000. She uses the investment to match a gain of £40,000, claiming £20,000 as reinvestment relief. In 2019 she receives value from the issuing company such that her income tax relief is reduced to £32,000. Her reinvestment relief is reduced accordingly:

$$\text{Reduction in relief} = £20{,}000 \times \frac{£50{,}000 - £32{,}000}{£50{,}000} = £7{,}200$$

Note that where there is a restriction because of an excessive investment, and also a reduction of income tax, both restrictions are applied, in that order.

Law: TCGA 1992, Sch. 5BB, para. 5

17.4 Identifying shares on a disposal

Shares are generally matched on a first-in first-out basis. In some circumstances it may transpire that an investor holds a mix of shares in the issuing company acquired on the same day that attracted:

- income tax relief only;
- both income tax relief and CGT reinvestment relief; or
- neither,

depending on the particular prevailing conditions at the time the respective share issues took place.

If this is the case then the shares disposed of must be carefully identified in accordance with the special identification rules referred to by TCGA 1992, Sch. 5BB, para. 8(4). This is the same as for income tax relief considered in **16.3.6**.

The identification rules are relatively easy to follow, and essentially provide that the shares are not pooled as normally, but are treated as being disposed of on a first-in first-out basis.

In circumstances where shares attracting different relief are acquired on the same day, the rules stipulate that shares to which no relief is attached are treated as being disposed of first, followed by shares only attracting income tax relief (but not reinvestment relief), and finally shares attracting both.

Law: TCGA 1992, Sch. 5BB, para. 8(4)

18. CGT disposal and loss relief

18.1 CGT exemption

18.1.1 Overview

Where the shares issued under SEIS are held until the end of Period A before being disposed of, there are provisions in TCGA 1992 which can exempt any gain arising from CGT, whilst allowing any losses (subject to adjustment). Ordinarily, a disposal which would be exempt if it produced a gain cannot be allowable if it in fact produces a loss. An example of this would be qualifying corporate bonds (QCBs).

Gains will only be exempt (or partly exempt) if income tax relief has been claimed and not wholly withdrawn. Special consideration needs to be given to circumstances where relief has been withdrawn in part – for example because of a part disposal before the termination date.

Law: TCGA 1992, s. 150E, 150F

18.1.2 Income tax relief to have been claimed

An essential requirement of the CGT exemption is that income tax relief must have been claimed on the relevant shares. It is not sufficient that relief was potentially available, there has to be at least some relief claimed by the investor. There has to be some reduction in income tax liability attributable to the SEIS investment.

This requirement was examined in *Ames*, where the taxpayer had invested in qualifying shares, but not made any claim to EIS income tax relief because his income did not exceed the personal allowance for the year in question. There was also no scope to carry back the relief. As it transpired the only way to have done so would have been for him to disclaim part of the personal allowance, and as he had not done this within the prerequisite time limits HMRC refused his claim, as they did not feel that he had a reasonable excuse (for the lateness).

Law: TCGA 1992, s. 150E(1)

Case: *Ames v HMRC* [2015] UKFTT 337 (TC)

18.1.3 Relief not withdrawn

Where income tax has been claimed and has not subsequently been withdrawn at all, a disposal after the end of Period A will be fully exempt in respect of the shares which attracted the SEIS income tax relief. In the situation where the original investment was greater than the permitted annual limit, the exemption is available on a pro rata basis (discussed below).

Example – full exemption

Jenna invests £100,000 in SEIS shares on 6 April 2014. The termination date relating to the shares is 6 April 2017. Jenna claims income tax relief and holds the shares for the required period. She sells the shares on 1 December 2019 for £200,000. The gain is exempt from CGT.

The disposal on which the exemption is being claimed should be included in the CGT summary pages on the tax return, with the relief then claimed to offset it, and an explanatory note inserted in the white space.

Law: TCGA 1992, s. 150E(2)

18.1.4 Relief partly withdrawn

If, following a qualifying investment, events transpire so that the original relief given is withdrawn in full, then any gain will be fully chargeable. The consideration will only be relevant if the shares continue to be held, so the only circumstances relevant when considering the partial availability of CGT relief are the receipt of value.

It is (hopefully) fairly obvious that CGT exemption cannot be granted on shares which were disposed of before the termination date!

There is no restriction on the CGT exemption if SEIS relief is not enjoyed in full solely because the individual did not have sufficient income tax liability to utilise the maximum relief available.

Example – partial income tax relief

Nadia subscribes for 100,000 shares at £1 each under EIS. Ordinarily the maximum relief would be £100,000 x 50% = £50,000; however her income tax liability for the year of investment and for the preceding year were £20,000 and £10,000 respectively. Utilising the carryback provision, her SEIS relief enjoyed was therefore £30,000. This partial enjoyment does not restrict Nadia's claim to the CGT exemption in itself.

If, however, during Period A there is a receipt of value leading to a reduction in relief, there will be a restriction on the CGT exemption.

The restriction will depend on the reduction in income tax relief that arose from the receipt of value. To calculate the amount of the gain that is no longer exempt, the following formula is used:

$$\text{Gain x } \frac{\text{The amount of reduction in income tax relief}}{\text{Total relief attributable to the shares}}$$

This is then deducted from the amount of the gain to find the remaining exempt part.

Example – value received

Suppose Nadia receives value of £50,000 during Period A. The reduction in SEIS income tax relief is £25,000. Now assume that she sells the shares after the termination date for £200,000 – i.e. a gain of £100,000. Of this the exempt amount is:

$$£100{,}000 - \left(£100{,}000 \text{ x } \frac{£25{,}000}{£50{,}000}\right) = £50{,}000$$

The remaining £50,000 is a chargeable gain.

A further complication occurs where there is both a reduction due to receipt of value or redemption/repayment of capital, and an investment in excess of the permitted annual maximum. This is discussed below.

Law: TCGA 1992, s. 150F

18.1.5 Other restrictions

Relief will be restricted in circumstances where the original investment exceeded the maximum permitted amount for a year. The current maximum annual investment amount is £100,000, so if an investor bought shares for £150,000, disposal relief would be restricted to two-thirds of any gain arising on a disposal – or two-thirds of the total gains on a series of disposals.

On each disposal, the gain arising is multiplied by the fraction given below to find the exemption:

$$\frac{\text{Income tax relief obtained}}{\text{SEIS rate x total amount invested}}$$

So in the case of the investor discussed above, a sale for £500,000 would give a total maximum exempt amount of:

$$£350{,}000 \text{ x } \frac{£50{,}000}{50\% \text{ x } £150{,}000} = £233{,}334$$

The remaining £116,666 of gain remains chargeable.

Law: TCGA 1992, s. 150E(4), (5)

Excess investment and reduction of relief

As discussed briefly above, a complicated situation arises where there is both an excessive initial investment (i.e. one which is in excess of the permitted annual maximum) and a reduction in income tax relief during Period A because of a receipt of value.

To determine correctly how much of any subsequent gain is exempt, the first step is to calculate the exempt gain following an excessive investment (so £233,334 in the case of the investor discussed above). This now becomes the maximum exempt gain. This figure then replaces the total gain figure used to determine the deduction in the formula given in **18.1.4** (i.e. calculating the restriction following a partial withdrawal of relief).

Representing this in formulaic form in full, this gives us:

$$\text{Gain (reduced)} - \left[\text{Gain (reduced) x } \frac{\text{The amount of reduction in income tax releif}}{\text{Total relief attributable to the shares}}\right]$$

where Gain (reduced) is:

$$\text{Total gain x } \frac{\text{Income tax relief obtained}}{\text{SEIS rate x total amount invested}}$$

A worked example is given at VCM 40090, reproduced below:

HMRC example

In this example TCGA92/S150E(2) applies and TCGA92/S150E(5) applies also to restrict the exemption.

- December 2012 investor subscribes £150,000 for 100,000 shares in a SEIS company. Maximum Income Tax relief of £50,000 is given in the tax year 2012-13 applying the SEIS rate 50%.
- January 2014 the investor receives £20,000 value from the company. The Income Tax relief is reduced by £6,666 (£10,000 x £100,000 / £150,000) by making an assessment.
- January 2018 all the shares are sold for £270,000.

The chargeable gain before any exemption under section 150E(2) is calculated:

Disposal proceeds	£270,000
Less cost	£150,000
Chargeable gain	£120,000

The TCGA92/S150E (5) formula is:

$$\frac{R}{T} = \frac{\text{Amount of tax relief}}{\text{Subscription x SEIS rate}} = \frac{£50,000}{£75,000}$$

The chargeable gain exemption is restricted to £120,000 x 2/3 = £80,000 leaving a chargeable gain at this point of £40,000.

The TCGA92/S150E (5) formula is:

$$\frac{A}{B} = \frac{\text{Reduction in relief}}{\text{Relief attributable to shares before the reduction}}$$

The exemption is further reduced by the following amount:

$$£80,000 \text{ x } \frac{£6,666}{£50,000} = £10,666$$

The exempt gain becomes £69,334 and the chargeable gain £50,666 (£40,000 + £10,666).

Law: TCGA 1992, s. 150E(2), (5)

Guidance: VCM 40090

18.2 Losses

18.2.1 Generally

As mentioned in the overview, in most circumstances where a disposal would be exempt from CGT if it produced a gain, any loss arising on such a disposal would be non-allowable. This works because the legislation specifically disapplies the provision preventing a disposal from being a chargeable event where a loss arises.

In calculating the loss, the allowable costs have to be reduced by the amount of income tax relief given and not subsequently withdrawn.

Example – restriction of capital loss

Pietro invests £100,000 in shares in a SEIS qualifying company, claiming the full £50,000 SEIS income tax relief. No relief is withdrawn. The shares eventually become worthless and the company is liquidated. The capital loss of £100,000 is reduced by the £50,000 income tax relief given and not withdrawn, meaning the allowable loss is £50,000.

In the event that there is only a part disposal, the reduction is made on a pro rata basis.

Example – restriction for part disposal

Thomas invests £100,000 in shares in a SEIS qualifying company, claiming the full £50,000 SEIS income tax relief, which is not subsequently withdrawn. He later sells half of the shares for £5,000. The loss of £45,000 is reduced by £25,000 (i.e. half of the income tax relief not withdrawn).

Law: TCGA 1992, s. 150E

18.2.2 Offsetting losses against general income

Losses arising on disposals of "qualifying shares" may be offset against general income rather than against other capital gains.

Unlike EIS shares, shares are not automatically qualifying shares for these purposes if SEIS relief is attributable to them. It is, however, highly likely that SEIS shares will qualify for share loss relief under the general provisions. Because the shares need to qualify in their own right, the company would need to continue trading after the termination date (unlike EIS shares which need only have attributable income tax relief not withdrawn).

Where losses are to be relieved against general income, they can be relieved against income for the year in which the loss arose, the preceding year, or both. It may be necessary to offset both the years' income if the loss exceeds the income for one of the years. If a claim is being made to relieve income in both tax years, the taxpayer should specify on his return which year is to be offset first.

There is a general restriction on sideways loss relief introduced by FA 2013. This restriction limits the maximum offset of the capital loss against income to the higher of:

- £50,000; or
- 25% of the taxpayer's income.

Losses arising on SEIS shares which are to be relieved against income do not fall within the provisions of this cap – found in ITA 2007, s. 24A – because restrictions are already imposed upon maximum investment amounts attracting relief. This is confirmed by s. 24A(7). Losses in excess of the general restriction limit can therefore be relieved in full provided that they are shares to which SEIS relief is attributable.

Having identified that share loss relief is available due to attributable SEIS relief, and that there is income to offset, normal procedures for claiming share loss relief should be followed (found in ITA 2007, s. 133).

If all of the loss cannot be relieved against income in the relevant two years (because there is not enough income to relieve the loss fully), the unused balance can be used against capital gains arising in the same year as the loss, or carried forward to offset future capital gains.

Law: ITA 2007, s. 24A, 131, 133

18.3 Reorganisations

18.3.1 Bonus issues

A bonus issue is an event where existing shareholders are given additional shares, usually calculated by reference to their existing holding (e.g. one new share for every two existing shares). Provided that the bonus issue is made in this way, the bonus shares will be treated as if they were acquired at the same time as the existing shares. The income tax relief attributable to each share is simply spread across more shares, and so the shares can qualify for the disposal relief in the event of a part disposal.

Law: ITA 2007, s. 257E(4)

18.3.2 Rights issues

In contrast, a rights issue is an opportunity (i.e. right) to participate in a further share issue in exchange for a subscription. The new shares are treated for the purposes of SEIS relief as a separate investment to the original shares, and so the qualifying conditions will need to be met at the time of the rights issue if SEIS income tax relief (and therefore disposal relief) is to apply.

Law: TCGA 1992, s. 150E(8)

18.3.3 Share exchanges

When another company wants to acquire the SEIS company, it may do so by purchasing all of the shares. This could lead to a withdrawal of income tax relief for the individual shareholders if it occurs before the termination date of the shares. A purchase in this way will also be a disposal for CGT purposes, and so the conditions necessary for disposal relief will need to be considered.

Alternatively, the acquiring company could take over the SEIS company by issuing its own shares in exchange for the existing share capital. The SEIS shareholders subsequently become shareholders in the parent company. The consequences for any income tax relief are discussed at **16.3.5**.

Ordinarily on a takeover actioned by a share exchange, the new shares are treated as standing in the shoes of the old shares, and no disposal is deemed to have taken place for CGT purposes. For exchanges involving SEIS shares, the general rule is that the exchange constitutes a disposal for CGT purposes (i.e. it is a chargeable event). Recall that if a disposal occurs before the termination date, disposal relief is not available.

This general rule (which disapplies TCGA 1992, s. 135-137) applies to any takeover of shares which were issued under SEIS, unless:

- all income tax relief obtained on the shares has been withdrawn (this could result from the takeover itself, if the conditions in ITA 2007, s. 247 are not met); or
- not all the income tax relief is withdrawn, but:
    - the exchange takes place after the third anniversary of the original share issue, and the conditions in (1) below are met, or
    - the conditions in (2) are met.

1. *Takeover by another SEIS company*

If:

- one SEIS qualifying company, that is a company which has issued one or more compliance certificates (SEIS3), takes over a second SEIS qualifying company; and
- the new holding consists of new ordinary shares issued by the acquiring SEIS company after the anniversary date referred to above that carry no present or future preferential rights to dividends or to assets on a winding up, and no present or future rights to be redeemed,

then the ordinary "no disposal" position set out in s. 135 will apply, provided that the anti-avoidance provisions in s. 137 (no tax avoidance motive etc.) are not applicable.

2. *Takeover by new parent company*

Where:

- a company, having issued only subscriber shares, acquires all the shares (and securities) in a SEIS company in exchange only for the proportionate issue of its own shares (and securities) of a corresponding description, that is carrying the same essential rights as the old shares; and
- before the issue of the new shares (and securities) HMRC have notified the new company or the old company that they are satisfied that the share exchange will take place for bona fide commercial reasons and will not form part of any such scheme or arrangements as are mentioned in TCGA 1992, s. 137,

no disposal is deemed to take place, and the shares stand in the place of the original shares.

Law: TCGA 1992, s. 150E (9), (10), (11), (13)

Social Investment Tax Relief

19. SITR: introduction to the relief

19.1 History

Social Investment Tax Relief (SITR) is the newest of the State aid type tax reliefs. The relief has been available for qualifying investments made on or after 6 April 2014 – i.e. tax years 2014-15 and later.

The relief was introduced as an acknowledgment by the then coalition Government of the increasing role played by social enterprises, both in the economy and in tackling social issues and problems. Prior to the introduction of the relief, such an organisation would have to use either EIS or VCT relief to try to attract investment through tax efficient means.

Following a period of consultation, SITR was introduced in FA 2014. It was originally in force for investments made up to 5 April 2019; however, this was extended to 5 April 2021 by *Finance (No. 2) Act* 2017.

EU Commission

SITR is compliant with EU State aid regulations for *de minimis* schemes, meaning it could be introduced without seeking specific EU approval.

This is far less onerous than the requirements that the EIS scheme needs to meet. However, it originally restricted the maximum amount that organisations can raise over a rolling three-year period. Following the expansion of the relief from April 2017, this restriction now only affects older enterprises.

Law: *Commission Regulation* 1407/2013

19.2 Tax relief

The operation of SITR is broadly based on the EIS scheme, and so the tax reliefs work in a similar way. There are three facets to the relief:

- income tax relief;
- CGT exemption; and
- CGT deferral relief.

A unique feature of SITR is that relief can be given on debt investments as well as equity – so an investor can make a loan (subject to qualifying conditions) to a social enterprise and claim relief.

There is no specific provision to allow share loss relief on SITR equity investments (see below).

19.2.1 Income tax relief

For qualifying investments, relief is given as a tax reduction against the overall liability for the tax year of the investment (or the preceding year). This is therefore applied after other reliefs, such as the personal allowance (if applicable) and personal pension contributions. The current rate of relief is 30% on up to £1 million per tax year. Like EIS, the relief cannot create a repayment (or further repayment) by reducing the overall tax liability below £nil.

Where the relief available exceeds the tax liability for the year of the investment, the possibility should be explored of carrying back some or all of the claim into the preceding tax year; however, relief cannot be carried back to a year earlier than 2014-15.

Law: ITA 2007, Pt. 5B

19.2.2 CGT exemption

Where a claim to SITR has been made successfully and not subsequently withdrawn, any gain arising on equity investments themselves will not be charged to CGT upon a disposal, provided the minimum holding period has elapsed.

Law: TCGA 1992, s. 255B

19.2.3 CGT deferral relief

Where a qualifying investment is made, the investor can match the amount invested to any capital gains realised in the period beginning three years prior to the SITR investment, and ending one year afterward. The CGT arising on that part of the gain is then deferred until the SITR shares are disposed of (or relief is cancelled).

However, gains arising prior to 6 April 2014 cannot be deferred using SITR.

Law: TCGA 1992, Sch. 8B

19.2.4 Loss relief

If shares invested via SITR are eventually sold at a loss, the loss will be allowable against other capital gains of the same year, or available to carry forward to offset future losses. There is no specific provision for SITR shares to qualify automatically for share loss relief (i.e. against general income); however, it is highly likely that shares will qualify under the general provisions in any case. Losses which do qualify for income tax relief are not restricted by the general cap on income tax reliefs.

There is no specific relief for debt investments, and so any loss realised is subject to normal CGT rules.

Law: ITA 2007, s. 131

19.3 Claiming relief - process

The way in which relief is secured for SITR broadly follows the methodology for EIS relief. The social enterprise initiates the process by completing the compliance statement SITR(2014), and sending this to HMRC. This gives details of the relevant investments, and key information about the social enterprise itself, all of which will allow HMRC to make a decision on whether the investments qualify. It is important for information on this form to be completely accurate, as making a false statement and declaration can attract a fine of up to £3,000.

It is possible for the social enterprise to request an informal, non-binding initial opinion from HMRC - known as an advanced assurance. This is not compulsory, but may be seen as attractive by potential investors. From January 2018, however, HMRC will not issue an opinion on any purely speculative investment - that is to say, in order to obtain an advance assurance, you will need to have details of all the prospective investors. You can no longer seek an advance assurance, and then use it as a catalyst to attract investors.

If HMRC agree that the investments qualify for the relief, they will grant a social enterprise the authority to issue compliance certificates to the investors, who can then claim the relevant relief. As for EIS, a claim for relief cannot be made before the certificates have been issued and received by the investor.

In order for the investor to claim tax relief, the relevant information should be entered in the self-assessment tax return where the investor is required to make such returns. Alternatively, if the investor is not registered for self-assessment, relief can be given via the PAYE code by writing to the address shown on the most recent PAYE coding notice, enclosing the compliance certificates received.

20. Conditions relating to the social enterprise

20.1 Introduction

For relief to be attributable to an investment, the body invested in must be a qualifying social enterprise. In this chapter we will consider what is meant by a social enterprise for these purposes, and the qualifying conditions related to it.

Shorter applicable period

Many of these conditions are expressed in relation to the "shorter applicable period". This is defined as the period that begins on the investment date, and ends on the third anniversary thereof.

Law: ITA 2007, s. 257KC

20.2 The conditions in detail

20.2.1 Social enterprise

Only qualifying social enterprises can offer investment relief. A qualifying social enterprise must be one or more of the following throughout the minimum holding period of the investment:

- a community interest company;
- a community benefit society, with an asset lock; or
- a charity (either a trust or a company).

An in-depth discussion of exactly what each of these vehicles is goes beyond the scope of this publication. It is likely, in any case, that organisations seeking to offer investments attracting SITR will be fully aware of whether they fall into one of these categories. We will instead focus on the additional requirements set out by the legislation.

Note that relief cannot be given under SITR if relief has already been given on the same investment by EIS, SEIS, or community investment tax relief.

Law: ITA 2007, s. 257J

20.2.2 Continuing to be a social enterprise

In order for the right to relief to be maintained, the social enterprise must remain a qualifying social enterprise throughout the shorter applicable period.

Law: ITA 2007, s. 257M

20.2.3 Maximum amount raised

Changes from April 2017

Finance (No. 2) Act 2017 introduces a lifetime limit of £1.5 million where either:

- the investment is made before the end of the period of seven years beginning with the first commercial sale; or
- the investment is made after the end of that period, but a relevant investment was made during the initial seven year period.

In practice, this means that the rolling three-year restriction will apply to any enterprise that doesn't raise funds through risk-finance (including EIS, SEIS or VCT) within seven years of its first commercial sale.

There are complex rules that apply where a company that has raised funds via SITR subsequently is acquired by, or transfers its trade to, another social enterprise. When applying the seven-year limit, the first commercial sale is the earliest sale of the enterprise itself, or any current or former subsidiary, or former owner of any acquired trade. The £1.5 million limit also applies collectively across this range of entities.

This is to prevent an enterprise from side-stepping the limit by acquiring a company or trade that has benefitted from social investments after the date the relevant investment is made

Prior to April 2017

Unlike EIS, up until April 2017 there was no lifetime limit on the amount that can be raised via SITR. Neither is there a maximum age restriction. However, there is a restriction on amounts that can be raised via SITR (or other *de minimis* State aid) measured over a three-year rolling period. This continues for older enterprises that do not qualify for the new lifetime limit discussed above.

For entities that do not qualify, this means that every time there is an investment which potentially qualifies for SITR, the amount raised via the relief or other *de minimis* State aid measures in the 36 months leading up to the investment date must be scrutinised carefully.

The permitted maximum amount is calculated by reference to a formula, which at first glance can appear complicated. The formula that must be applied is:

$$\left[\frac{€200{,}000 - M}{RCG + RSI}\right] - T$$

where:

M = the total of any other *de minimis* aid received in the three years prior to the investment.

RCG = the highest rate of capital gains tax in the three years prior to the investment.

RSI = the highest rate of SITR income tax relief in the three years prior to the investment.

T = the total of any other SITR investments made in the three years prior to investment.

Example

Charity Ltd is a qualifying social enterprise. On 6 April 2018 it is looking to raise some funds via SITR. It has received no previous funding via this initiative; however it has received €50,000 via other *de minimis* State aid within the previous three years. The maximum amount it can raise via its investment round is:

$$\frac{€200{,}000 - €50{,}000}{28\% + 30\%} = €258{,}620$$

It is essential to note that when working out the maximum permitted amount of investment, the result is given in Euros not sterling. Spot rates at the date of investment should be used, not averages for any particular period.

If the amount the enterprise is looking to raise exceeds the amount calculated by the formula it will need to restrict the amounts raised via SITR accordingly.

Law: ITA 2007, s. 257MA, 257MNA, 257MNC, 257MND

20.2.4 Gross assets

The gross assets of the social enterprise (or amalgamated gross assets of a group if the social enterprise is a parent company) must not exceed:

- £15 million immediately before the relevant investment; or
- £16 million immediately after the relevant investment.

Gross assets refer to the value (before deducting any liabilities) of any property the enterprise owns that would appear on the balance sheet were it to draw one up on the investment date. The valuation method cannot be altered from that used to prepare the most recent financial statements – so an artificially depressed value cannot be achieved through (say) a change in depreciation policy.

In the case of groups, any intra group balances are disregarded.

Law: ITA 2007, s. 257MC

20.2.5 Unquoted status

At the time of the investment, the social enterprise must be not be a quoted company; that is to say, its shares must not be listed on a recognised stock exchange if it is in fact a company. AIM listed shares are treated as unquoted for these purposes.

As well as meeting this condition at the time of investment, there must be no existing arrangements for the social enterprise to become a quoted company, or to become a subsidiary of another company which is quoted (or will be subject to existing arrangements).

Law: ITA 2007, s. 257MD

20.2.6 Control and independence

At no point during the shorter applicable period may the social enterprise (alone or with any connected persons) control any subsidiaries which are not "qualifying subsidiaries" (see below).

Additionally, the social enterprise must be independent; that is to say, it must not itself be under the control of another company – whether alone or with any persons connected to that company.

There must be no arrangements in place at any time during the shorter applicable period that would result in either of these conditions not being met at any time.

Law: ITA 2007, s. 257ME

20.2.7 Qualifying subsidiaries

There is a specific condition (which oddly seems to be identical to the previous condition!) that if the social enterprise has any subsidiaries during the shorter applicable period, they must be qualifying subsidiaries.

A subsidiary qualifies if:

- the subsidiary is a 51% subsidiary of the parent,
- no person other than the parent, or another of its subsidiaries, has control of the subsidiary, and
- no arrangements are in existence as a result of which either of the conditions would cease to be met.

Law: ITA 2007, s. 257MF

20.2.8 Property management subsidiaries

This is an extension to the general condition. If any of the social enterprise's subsidiaries carry on a business which is mainly that of holding land, or property deriving value from land, that subsidiary has to be a 90% subsidiary (rather than just a 51% subsidiary).

Law: ITA 2007, s. 257MG

20.2.9 Number of employees

At the time of the investment, the social enterprise (or group as a whole where applicable) must have no more than 250 full time equivalent employees (including directors). The limit was 500 for investments made before 6 April 2017.

Full time for this purpose means an employee who normally works at least 35 hours per week.

Part time employees need to be accounted for, and in doing so their hours need to be aggregated together. For example, two employees who both work 17.5 hours per week together constitute one single full time equivalent for the purpose of the limit.

Only employees who are still working for the social enterprise at the issue date need to be accounted for – so seasonal staff may not need to be counted. Neither do staff absent on maternity or paternity leave, or students away on vocational training.

Note that volunteers do not count toward this limit.

Law: ITA 2007, s. 257MH

20.2.10 No partnerships

During the shorter applicable period, neither the social enterprise nor any 90% subsidiary of the social enterprise is permitted to be a member of a partnership.

Law: ITA 2007, s. 257MI

20.2.11 Trading requirement

The trading requirement must be met throughout the shorter applicable period. As a reminder, this begins with the date of the investment, and ends on the third anniversary of that investment.

There is an exception to meeting this requirement where the social enterprise is an accredited social impact contractor. These are special purpose vehicles which are set up to target specific social issues, for example poverty or environmental protection. In order to qualify an accreditation process must be passed and approved by the Cabinet office. It is likely that most investments practitioners will advise on will not fall into this category.

The trading requirement will be met if:

- the social enterprise is a charity; or
- the social enterprise is a single company that is not a charity and:
    - any non-trade activities are merely incidental, and
    - any excluded activities do not form a substantial part of the overall business activities; or

- the social enterprise is a parent company that is not a charity and the business of the group as a whole does not consist to a substantial part in the carrying on of non-qualifying activities.

Non-trade activities will include investment type activities, such as a rental business. There is a specific list of excluded activities. As for other reliefs, substantial is taken to mean broadly 20% of all activities.

Law: ITA 2007, s. 257MJ

Excluded activities

Excluded activities are listed under section 257MQ of ITA 2007, (reproduced below):

> "The following are excluded activities for the purposes of sections 257JD, 257MJ and 257MP–
>
> (a) dealing in land, in commodities or futures or in shares, securities or other financial instruments,
>
> (b) banking, insurance, money-lending, debt-factoring, hire-purchase financing or other financial activities (but see subsection (2)),
>
> (ba) leasing (including letting ships on charter or other assets on hire,
>
> (bb) receiving royalties or licence fees,
>
> (bc) operating or managing nursing homes or residential care homes or managing property used as a nursing home or residential care home,
>
> (bd) generating electricity, exporting electricity or making electricity generating capacity available,
>
> (be) generating heat,
>
> (bf) generating any form of energy not within paragraph (bd) or (be),
>
> (bg) producing gas or fuel,

(c) property development (see section 257MR),

(d) activities in the fishery and aquaculture sector that is covered by Council Regulation (EC) No. 104/2000 of 17 December 1999 on the common organisation of the markets in fishery and aquaculture products,

(e) the primary production of products listed in Annex I to the Treaty on the Functioning of the European Union (agricultural etc products), with the exception of products covered by Council Regulation (EC) No. 104/2000(fishery and aquaculture products),

(f) [replaced by (bd) to (bg) from April 2017 onward],

(g) road freight transport for hire or reward, and

(h) providing services or facilities for a business carried on by another person (other than a company of which the provider of the services or facilities is a qualifying subsidiary) if–

  (i) the business consists wholly or as to a substantial part of activities falling within any of paragraphs (a) to (g), and

  (ii) a controlling interest (see section 257MT) in the business is held by a person who also has a controlling interest in the business carried on by the provider of the services or facilities."

Law: ITA 2007, s. 257MJ

Administration

The social enterprise will not be treated as ceasing to meet the trading requirement during the shorter relevant period merely because it, or any of its subsidiaries, enters administration or receivership. However, the entering into administration or receivership and everything done as a result must have occurred for genuine commercial reasons, and not as part of arrangements related to tax avoidance.

Law: ITA 2007, s. 257MK

20.2.12 *Trade to be carried out by social enterprise*

During the shorter relevant period, the qualifying trade referred to above has to be carried on by the social enterprise, or a qualifying 90% subsidiary of it. There is an exception to this where the social enterprise or 90% subsidiary ceases to carry on the relevant trade due to entering administration or receivership, or is dissolved or wound up for genuine commercial reasons, and following this the trade is carried on by a person unconnected to the social enterprise.

Law: ITA 2007, s. 257MN

20.2.13 *Use of money raised*

The money raised via SITR investments has to be used for the purpose of the qualifying trade (as discussed above), or preparatory work undertaken to commence such a trade which is then so commenced within two years from the investment date.

All of the funds raised must be employed wholly for the use of the funded purpose – that is, the qualifying trade or preparatory work. As for EIS, there is a small exception for insignificant amounts which are not so employed.

No relief can be granted until the chosen trade, whether that be the qualifying trade or the preparatory work intended to lead to one, has been carried out for at least four months.

There are further let outs here where the failure to employ the funds is due to entering receivership or administration, with the same conditions as for the previous sections regarding commercial reasoning etc.

From 6 April 2017, the money will not be considered to have been employed for the purposes of the qualifying trade if it is used to repay or refinance existing loans.

Law: ITA 2007, s. 257MM

20.2.14 *Financial health*

For investments made on or after 6 April 2017, a social enterprise which is in difficulty cannot use SITR to raise funds. "In difficulty" for these purposes means that it would be regarded as a firm in difficulty for the purposes of the Community Guidelines on State Aid for Rescuing and Restructuring Firms in Difficulty.

Law: ITA 2007, s. 257MIA

21. Conditions relating to the investor and investment

21.1 Introduction

We will now turn to look at conditions relating to the investment generally, and conditions which must be met by the investor.

It should be noted that there is no requirement for the investor to be UK resident. In order to utilise the relief, however, he or she will need to have a UK income tax liability.

An individual investor can claim SITR on investment of up to £1 million in any tax year. However, the restriction of the amount that a single social enterprise may raise must be borne in mind, and so investors wishing to make substantial investments will need to make multiple investments.

Law: ITA 2007, Pt. 5B, Ch. 3

21.2 Nature of the investment

21.2.1 Overview

At all times during the shorter applicable period (see **20.1**), the investment must be in either new shares which meet one of two conditions, or new qualifying debt investments. These are considered in turn below.

Law: ITA 2007, s. 257L

21.2.2 New shares

The shares must be new shares, i.e. must not be second-hand. These must be fully paid up in cash at the time the investment is made, in a similar way to EIS. Additionally, the shares must meet both condition A and B throughout the shorter applicable period.

Condition A is that the shares must not carry:

- a right to a fixed amount of return;
- a right to a fixed rate of return;
- a right of return which is fixed by reference to the investment amount;

- a right of return which is fixed by reference to something else which is irrespective of the financial success of the social enterprise; or
- a right to a return which exceeds a reasonable commercial rate for a similar investment.

If these rights are applicable in part – for example if shares carry a return which is partially fixed – the condition will not be met.

Example

Andy buys shares on which he intends to claim SITR. The shares carry a right guaranteeing a dividend identical to all of the share classes, plus 1% of the amount invested. This is sufficient to fail Condition A.

Condition B is that, in the event of a winding up, the shares carry rights in respect of amounts due to the holders which:

- rank after all debts of the social enterprise, except those due to holders of qualifying debt instruments on which SITR has been claimed; and
- do not rank above any other shares in the social enterprise.

Law: ITA 2007, s. 257L, 257LA

21.2.3 Debt investments

One of the big attractions of SITR is the ability to make a debt investment rather than equity one. This may be attractive to prospective investors because they do not need to rely on a third party to purchase the investment from them when they want to realise the amount invested; though of course a debt instrument can be sold to such a third party if desirable.

For a debt investment to be a qualifying debt investment for the purposes of SITR, it must be a debenture of the social enterprise in which the following conditions are met:

- neither the debt principal nor any return on it is secured by a charge on any of the social enterprise's assets, e.g. property;
- any rate of return carried by the debenture is not greater than a reasonable commercial rate of return;

- if the social enterprise is wound up, any sums due in respect of the debenture (both the initial principal investment and any rate of return owed but unpaid):
    - rank below all of the debts of the social enterprise, and equally to other unsecured debentures; and
    - rank equally with all shares in the social enterprise, except for those shares which rank above the other ordinary shares.

In practice, the last point means that the debenture has to rank equally with the lowest ranked share capital if there is any.

The actual form of the debenture is irrelevant as long as these conditions are met. It could therefore be an ordinary loan, loan notes, or any other form of debt. The key is that some money is actually lent. This can be as a single payment or as part of a series of payments. This will have an effect on when the investment is treated as being made (see below).

Law: ITA 2007, s. 257L

21.2.4 *When is the investment made?*

In the case of shares, the investment is made when the investor becomes entitled to the rights attaching to the shares. This is exactly the same as under EIS, and in most cases will be the share subscription date.

In the case of a debt investment, the investment will be treated as being made when the money is actually transferred to the social enterprise, unless the loan agreement does not take effect until later on, in which case the investment will be treated as being made on the date the loan agreement commences. If the investment results in debentures being issued by the social enterprise, then the investment will be treated as being made when the debentures are actually issued.

Where the debt investment consists of a series of transactions, each transaction is treated as a separate investment, unless they relate to an issue of debentures or commencement of a loan agreement which takes place after the date of the separate investments.

Law: ITA 2007, s. 257LA

21.3 No pre-arranged exits

It is intended that investors participate in the social enterprise on a full risk basis. This would not be the case if there were arrangements in place which safeguarded their position over and above the generous tax relief. SITR therefore does not apply to any investments where, during the shorter applicable period, there exist:

(a) arrangements with a view to the subsequent repurchase, exchange or other disposal of those shares or of other shares in or securities of the social enterprise;

(b) arrangements for or with a view to the cessation of any trade which is being (or is to be, or may be) carried on by the social enterprise or a person connected with that company; or

(c) arrangements for the disposal of, or of a substantial amount (in terms of value) of, the assets of the social enterprise or of a person connected with it.

Arrangements will not be caught by this provision is if they merely relate to arrangements for the winding up of the social enterprise, unless these arrangements were part of the issuing arrangements.

Law: ITA 2007, s. 257LB

21.4 No risk avoidance

During the shorter applicable period, there must be no arrangements, the main purpose or one of the main purposes of which is (by means of any insurance, indemnity or guarantee or otherwise) to provide partial or complete protection for persons investing in the social enterprises against what would otherwise be the risks attached to making the investment.

Arrangements for these purposes do not include those which are undertaken:

- for the social enterprise itself; or
- if the social enterprise is a parent company that meets the trading requirement, or is a parent company that is an accredited social impact contractor:

- for the social enterprise itself,
- for the social enterprise itself and one or more of its subsidiaries, or
- for one or more of the subsidiaries of the social enterprise.

This would therefore prevent investments from failing to qualify for relief purely because, for example, the social enterprise takes out a public liability insurance policy with a view to protecting its own assets in the event of legal action.

Law: ITA 2007, s. 257LC

21.5 No linked loans

No relief will be given under SITR if, during the shorter applicable period, the investor receives a loan which in the absence of an investment:

- would not have been made; or
- would not have been made on the same terms.

As for EIS, it is not necessary that the loan is made by the social enterprise to fail this condition, just that the loan needs to be linked somehow to the investment. So if the loan is an ordinary bank loan, but carries a charge on shares subscribed for in the social enterprise, the loan will be linked, and the investment will not qualify for relief.

Law: ITA 2007, s. 257LD

21.6 Employees, etc.

21.6.1 Introduction

As with the other EIS reliefs, there are conditions which must be met in terms of the investor's relationship with the social enterprise. The first of these relates to employee type relationships.

The period in which such relationships must be looked at is referred to as the "longer applicable period".

21.6.2 The longer applicable period

This is the period which commences on:

(a) the day on which the social enterprise is:

 (i) incorporated (if it is a body corporate); or

 (ii) established (in any other case), or

(b) if later, the day whose first anniversary is the investment date.

So the period can extend back to one year prior to the investment. The period ends on the third anniversary of the investment.

21.6.3 Details of exclusions

No relief under SITR can be given if, in the longer applicable period, the investor or any of their associates is:

- an employee of:
    - the social enterprise;
    - a subsidiary of the social enterprise;
    - a partner of the social enterprise; or
    - a partner of a subsidiary of the social enterprise.
- a partner of:
    - the social enterprise; or
    - a subsidiary of the social enterprise.
- a trustee of:
    - the social enterprise; or
    - a subsidiary of the social enterprise.
- a paid director of:
    - the social enterprise; or
    - a subsidiary of the social enterprise.

This is broadly similar to the exclusions for EIS. The legislation confirms that where a director is also an employee concurrently, he or she is treated as only being a director.

21.6.4 *Payments that can be ignored*

A number of payments are ignored when considering whether a director is remunerated or not. These are:

- reimbursements of expenses incurred wholly, exclusively and necessarily by the individual in their duties as a director;
- payments of interest not exceeding a commercial rate on monies lent to the company;
- dividends which represent a normal return on the investment;
- payment for supplies of goods not exceeding market value;
- rent not exceeding a commercial level;
- payments for services provided by the individual that will form part of his trading profits for tax purposes, provided the services are not secretarial or managerial, and are not services which the enterprise itself provides;
- conditionally, other reasonable remuneration (see below).

Law: ITA 2007, s. 257LF

Reasonable remuneration

Directors may receive "reasonable" remuneration for services they provide (in their capacity as a director) provided that Condition A or (if applicable) Condition B is met. This mirrors the business angel exception under EIS.

Condition A is that:

- the director has never been connected with the social enterprise (at any time); and
- he or she has never been involved in carrying on any part of the trade or business of the social enterprise or of one of its subsidiaries.

Condition B is only relevant where there has been a previous investment. Condition B is that:

- the current investment does not meet condition A, but a previous investment did; and
- the current investment takes place before the third anniversary of the previous investment (i.e. the one for which condition A was met)

Law: ITA 2007, s. 257LF(6), (7)

21.7 Interest in share capital etc.

No relief can be given if, at any time during the longer applicable period (see **21.6**), the investor (or any associate of his) directly or indirectly possesses (or becomes entitled to possess):

- more than 30% of the ordinary share capital of a related company;
- more than 30% of the loan capital of a related company; or
- more than 30% of the voting power in a related company.

These provisions are ignored if the only time where the 30% of share capital limit is breached is where the investor holds original subscriber shares, and the company has not commenced trading.

Loan capital is defined as any debt incurred by the company for any money borrowed or capital assets acquired by the company, for any right to receive income created in favour of the company, or for consideration the value of which to the company was (at the time when the debt was incurred) substantially less than the amount of the debt including any premium.

Bank overdrafts are ignored when looking at loan capital.

Law: ITA 2007, s. 257LG

21.8 No collusion

No relief can be given if the investor or an associate, during the longer applicable period, is party to arrangements which provide for a non-qualifying investor to make an investment into a company other than the social enterprise.

Law: ITA 2007, s. 257LH

21.9 No tax avoidance

The investment must not be made as part of any arrangements the main purpose, or one of the main purposes, of which is the avoidance of tax.

Law: ITA 2007, s. 257LE

21.10 Existing investments

For investments made on or after 6 April 2017, an investor must be independent of the enterprise into which he or she is investing. This means that the investor cannot have an existing investment (either as a shareholder or debt-holder). There are a number of exceptions to this, and a pre-existing investment will not preclude SITR if:

- it consists of a loan, and SITR was claimed on the whole amount;
- it consists of shares, and relief under EIS, SEIS or SITR has been claimed on the whole amount subscribed; or
- the shares are "permitted subscriber shares".

The shares will only be permitted subscriber shares if they were:

- issued to the investor at the time the enterprise was incorporated, and the investor has held them ever since; or
- issued to the investor at a time when the issuing company:
- had issued no shares other than subscriber shares, and
- had not begun to carry or a trade, or undertake preparations to carry one on.

Law: ITA 2007, s. 257LDA

21.11 Disqualifying arrangements

Another new condition applying to investments made on or after 6 April 2017 is that the investment must not be made, and the money raised must not be employed, in consequence, anticipation or otherwise in connection with disqualifying arrangements. This mirrors the EIS provision.

Arrangements will be disqualifying if the main purpose, or one of the main purposes, of them is that the social enterprise, or a 90% subsidiary, will carry out a qualifying activity, and that as a result of an investment an individual will obtain tax relief, and either condition A or B is met.

Condition A is that as a result (direct or indirect) of the money raised by the share issue, all or most of that money (or an equivalent amount) is subsequently paid to or for the benefit of a relevant person or persons.

A relevant person is one who is party to the arrangements, or someone connected to such a person.

Condition B is applicable in circumstances where, in the absence of the arrangements, it would have been reasonable to expect that the whole or greater part of the component activities of the relevant business activity would have been carried on as part of another business by a person or by persons who are party to the arrangements or a person or persons connected with such a party.

Law: ITA 2007, s. 257LEA

22. Withdrawal of relief

22.1 Overview

A number of circumstances can arise which lead to SITR being withdrawn, or reduced. The circumstances are broadly similar to the withdrawal provisions under EIS and SEIS; and so may be familiar from those sections of this publication.

22.2 Disposals

22.2.1 Restriction of relief

If the investor makes a disposal of the investment before the end of the shorter applicable period (i.e. before the third anniversary of the investment date: see **20.1**), relief will be either withdrawn or reduced depending on the circumstances. Relief is not withdrawn if the disposal is to a spouse or civil partner who lives with the investor, or occurs upon the death the investor.

If the disposal takes place otherwise than as a bargain at arm's-length, relief is withdrawn in full, regardless of the level of any proceeds received.

Where the disposal is a bargain at arm's-length, the relief must be reduced by reference to the amount of proceeds received. The formula used to calculate how much relief is to be withdrawn is:

$$C \times R$$

where:

C is the amount of value or consideration received by the investor for the qualifying investment; and

R is the rate at which relief was initially given (currently 30%).

The reduction is subject to a maximum of the total relief attributable to the shares or debt investment disposed of – i.e. if these are sold at a gain the reduction is capped, and is simply withdrawn in full.

Law: ITA 2007, s. 257R

22.2.2 Relief not obtained in full

It may be that upon making a qualifying investment, the investor is unable to obtain maximum relief potentially attributable to the shares or qualifying debt investments. This may be, for example, because the investor does not have sufficient income tax liability to utilise the relief fully.

Where this happens, and there is a subsequent disposal of the investments prior to the third anniversary of the investment date, relief is reduced by calculating the reduction in the normal way, and then multiplying the result by the fraction:

$$\frac{\text{Actual amount of relief claimed}}{\text{Maximum potential relief}}$$

Example

William invests £1 million into qualifying social enterprise shares on 1 April 2018. The maximum potential relief is £300,000. However, he only has £200,000 of income tax liability to reduce and this is what he claims. The shares are sold for £800,000 on 1 April 2019. The amount of relief that must be withdrawn is:

$$\frac{200{,}000}{300{,}000} \text{ x £800,000 x 30\% = £160,000}$$

Law: ITA 2007, s. 257RA

22.2.3 Investments becoming subject to options

If the relevant investments become subject to either a put or call option during the relevant period, this will also be treated as a disposal and all relief will be withdrawn.

A call option is one which would bind the investor to sell the investments to the option holder, or other nominated person.

A put option is one which would bind the grantor of the option to purchase the investments. In theory this could take place prior to the shares being issued, and so the period under scrutiny is the longer applicable period.

Law: ITA 2007, s. 257RB, 257RC

22.2.4 Identification of investments on disposal

In some circumstances it may transpire that an investor holds a mix of investments in the social enterprise:

- acquired on the same day or different days; and/or
- that attracted either income tax relief, CGT deferral relief, both, or neither, depending on the particular prevailing conditions at the time the respective investments took place.

If this is the case then the investments disposed of must be carefully identified in accordance with the special identification rules set out in ITA 2007, s. 257TA.

The identification rules are relatively easy to follow, and essentially provide that the investments are not pooled as normally, but are treated as being disposed of on a first-in first-out basis. In circumstances where investments attracting different relief are acquired on the same day, the rules stipulate that investments to which no relief is attached are treated as being disposed of first, followed by investments only attracting deferral relief, shares only attracting income tax relief, and finally investments attracting both.

Law: ITA 2007, s. 257TA

22.3 Value received

22.3.1 Overview

Relief will be reduced if, in the longer applicable period, an investor (or any of his associates) receives value from the social enterprise, or any person connected with the social enterprise. The amount by which the relief is reduced is calculated in a similar way as for a premature disposal (see **22.2** above), with the amount of value received replacing the consideration in the formula.

Law: ITA 2007, s. 257Q

22.3.2 When is value received?

S257QE sets out the circumstances in which the investor will be considered as having received value:

"257QE(2)The investor receives value from the social enterprise at any time when the social enterprise–

(a) repays, redeems or repurchases any investments in the social enterprise which belong to the investor, or makes any payment to the investor for giving up the investor's right to investments in the social enterprise on their cancellation or extinguishment,

(b) repays, in pursuance of any arrangements for or in connection with the making of the investment, any debt owed to the investor other than a debt which was incurred by the social enterprise–

   (i) on or after the investment date, and

   (ii) otherwise than in consideration of the extinguishment of a debt incurred before that date,

(c) makes to the investor any payment for giving up on its extinguishment the investor's right to any debt, other than–

   (i) a debt in respect of a repayment of the kind mentioned in section 257LF(5)(a) or (f), or

   (ii) an ordinary trade debt,

(d) releases or waives any liability of the investor to the social enterprise or discharges or undertakes to discharge any liability of the investor to a third person,

(e) makes a loan or advance to the investor which has not been repaid in full before the investment is made,

(f) provides a benefit or facility for the investor by providing, at a price less than the arm's-length price or free of charge, goods or services for whose provision the social enterprise ordinarily makes a charge,

(g) otherwise provides any benefit or facility for the investor,

(h) transfers an asset to the investor for no consideration or for consideration less than its market value or acquires an asset from the investor for consideration greater than its market value, or

(i) makes to the investor any other payment except–

(i) a payment of a kind mentioned in section 257LF(5), or

(ii) a payment in discharge of an ordinary trade debt.

The payments mentioned in (h)(i)(i) above are those which are ignored when considering whether a director is remunerated or not [see **21.6.4**]."

Once it is established that value is received, it is necessary to quantify the amount so that the reduction can be calculated accurately. The table in **5.5.2** above details how to do this for EIS, and the principle here is the same. Please therefore refer to that table to determine amounts accordingly.

Law: ITA 2007, s. 257QE

22.3.3 Insignificant receipts

Value received will be ignored if it is insignificant. Insignificant means either:

- less than £1,000; or
- if more than £1,000, insignificant compared to the amount subscribed by the individual for the relevant shares.

If reliance is to be sought on the second point, then a subjective test will need to be carried out and agreement reached with HMRC.

Law: ITA 2007, s. 257QA

22.3.4 Replacement value

Where value has been received, there is scope for the investor to return the value to the person that it was received from. This is referred to as replacement value. If the value was received by an associate, it is the associate who must return the value rather than the individual. Similarly, if the payment was made not by the social enterprise but by a connected person, the return of value must go to that person.

In order for the provision to apply, the amount received must be returned in full – there is no credit given for a part return.

Where it is accepted that the value has been replaced, there will accordingly be no withdrawal or reduction of relief.

Law: ITA 2007, s. 257QH

22.4 Repayments of share capital

SITR enjoyed by the investor may be withdrawn if, during the longer applicable period, the company redeems or repurchases shares from:

- any shareholder, other than the investor; or
- a person to whom the repayment results in a reduction or withdrawal of SITR under the disposal or receipt of value provisions.

The relief can be partial depending on the amount paid to the other shareholder(s).

The rule also applies if a subsidiary company is the one that repurchases the shares, even if it did not become a subsidiary until after the transaction had taken place.

The total amount of withdrawal is calculated by multiplying the SITR rate by the amount of the capital repayment. This withdrawal then has to be divided between any SITR investment holders in an appropriate proportion relative to the relief they claimed. As can be seen, therefore, if the total capital repayment exceeds the total amount subscribed via SITR (in respect of investments when the third anniversary of the investment date has not yet passed), relief will be withdrawn in full.

Note that this provision applies throughout the longer applicable period, and so any share repurchases in the 12 months prior to any prospective SITR investment would need to be considered.

A repayment can be ignored as insignificant if the actual amount paid, as well as the market value of the shares it is paid in respect of, are insignificant. There is no stated threshold in the legislation, and HMRC therefore interpret insignificant as meaning trifling or unimportant.

The insignificant let out cannot be relied upon if the receipt is subject to any arrangements that were in existence in the 12 months prior to the investment date.

If the investor did not enjoy the maximum potential relief on the investment, the reduction will be restricted in the same way as discussed at **22.2** above.

Law: ITA 2007, s. 257QJ

22.5 Acquisition of trade or share capital

Relief under SITR will be withdrawn if a trade, or the majority of the assets used to carry out a trade, is acquired by the social enterprise, and at any time during the longer applicable period, the individual (together or with another group of individuals):

- owned more than a half share in the trade (unincorporated businesses); or
- controlled the company that previously carried on the trade (where the trade is carried on by a company).

As is often the case, the interests of any associated persons are aggregated with those of the individual for these purposes.

If the individual is a paid director, the time period is extended to any time before the end of the longer applicable period – i.e. no relief can be given if the director had more than a half share in a trade, or controlled the trading company, at any time before the end of the longer applicable period.

Relief will also be withdrawn if, during the longer applicable period, the social enterprise acquires shares in a company that the investor previously controlled.

Law: ITA 2007, s. 257QQ, 257QR

22.6 Social enterprise or investor ceases to qualify

Relief will be withdrawn if, prior to the third anniversary of the investment date, the social enterprise ceases to be a qualifying social enterprise, or the investor ceases to be qualifying investor.

The investor would cease to be a qualifying investor, for example, if he became interested in more than 30% of the ordinary share capital during the longer applicable period. The social enterprise would cease to be qualifying if, for example, it ceased to carry on a qualifying activity. Please refer to the previous two chapters for an in-depth discussion on the qualifying conditions.

22.7 Relief found not to have been due

HMRC have the power to withdraw relief where the company does not give notice of ceasing to meet any of the conditions and, in an officer's opinion, the requirements discussed in **Chapter 21** are not satisfied.

The officer must give notice to the social enterprise (not the investor), stating the reason why HMRC intend to withdraw the relief.

Law: ITA 2007, s. 257QS

23. Note on CGT reliefs

23.1 Overview

There is a large amount of overlap between the qualifying conditions for income tax relief and those for CGT deferral and disposal relief. The focus of this chapter is therefore on the differences, and readers will be referred back to previous points discussed where relevant.

23.2 CGT disposal relief

23.2.1 General principles

The legislation provides that if assets, to which an amount of SITR is attributable and has been claimed, are disposed of, any gain will not be a chargeable gain for CGT purposes.

Any loss arising will be an allowable loss. However, the sales proceeds will be reduced by the amount of SITR that has not been withdrawn.

The legislation closely follows the EIS provisions, and therefore there must be some actual reduction of income tax liability for the disposal relief to apply. It is not enough that the investor could have qualified for SITR but did not make a claim, for example because he had no income tax liability. See **6.1.2** for further discussion.

If the SITR has been fully withdrawn, any gain arising will be chargeable, and any losses arising will be not need to be restricted.

Law: TCGA 1992, s. 255A, 255B

23.2.2 Relief partly withdrawn

The CGT exemption will however be restricted where relief has been withdrawn:

- due to receipt of value; or
- due to redemption or repayment of share capital made to other shareholders.

There is no restriction on CGT exemption if SITR is not enjoyed in full solely because the individual did not have sufficient income tax liability to utilise the maximum relief available.

Example

Amy subscribes for 300,000 shares at £1 each under SITR. Ordinarily the maximum relief would be £300,000 x 30% = £90,000. However, her income tax liability for the year of investments and preceding year were £20,000 and £30,000 respectively. Utilising the carryback provision, her SITR relief enjoyed was therefore £50,000. This partial enjoyment does not restrict a claim to the CGT exemption in itself.

If, however, during the longer applicable period there is a receipt of value, or redemption/repayment of share capital leading to a reduction in relief, there will be a restriction on the CGT exemption.

The restriction will depend on the reduction in income tax relief that arose from the receipt of value, or redemption/repayment accordingly. To calculate the amount of the gain that is no longer exempt, the following formula is used:

$$\text{Gain x } \frac{\text{The amount of reduction in income tax relief}}{\text{Total relief attributable to the shares}}$$

This is then deducted from the amount of the gain to find the exempt part.

Example

Suppose Amy receives value of £50,000 during Period A. The reduction in SITR income tax relief is £15,000. Now assume she sells the shares after the end of the necessary investment period for £500,000 – i.e. a gain of £200,000. Of this the exempt amount is £200,000 – (£200,000 x £15,000/£50,000) = £140,000. The remaining £60,000 is a chargeable gain.

A further complication occurs where there is both a reduction due to receipt of value or redemption/repayment of capital, and an investment in excess of the permitted annual maximum. This is discussed at **23.2.4** below.

Law: TCGA 1992, s. 255D

23.2.3 Excess investments

Relief will be restricted in circumstances where the original investment exceeded the maximum permitted amount for a year. The current maximum annual investment amount is £1 million per individual, so if an investor made investments of £2 million, disposal relief would be restricted to half of any gain arising on a disposal – or half of the total gains on a series of disposals.

On each disposal, the gain arising is multiplied by the fraction given below to find the exemption:

$$\frac{\text{Income tax relief obtained}}{\text{SITR rate x total amount invested}}$$

So in the case of the investor discussed above, a sale for £5 million would give a total maximum exempt amount of:

$$\text{£3 million x } \frac{\text{£300,000}}{\text{30\% x £2 million}} = \text{£1.5 million}$$

The remaining £1.5 million of gain remains chargeable.

23.2.4 Excess investment and partial withdrawal

As discussed above briefly, a complicated situation arises where there is both an excessive initial investment (i.e. one which is in excess of the permitted annual maximum) and the reduction in income tax relief during the longer applicable period because of, for example, a receipt of value.

To determine correctly how much of any subsequent gain is exempt, the methodology to determine the exempt gain following an excessive investment should be followed first, so from our discussion above the result is £1.5 million. This now becomes the maximum exempt gain. This figure then replaces the total gain figure used to determine the deduction in the formula given in 23.2.1 (i.e. calculating the restriction following a partial withdrawal of relief).

Representing this in formulaic form in full, this gives us:

$$\text{Gain (reduced)} - \left[\text{Gain (reduced) x } \frac{\text{The amount of reduction in income tax relief}}{\text{Total relief attributable to the shares}}\right]$$

where Gain (reduced) is:

$$\text{Total gain x } \frac{\text{Income tax relief obtained}}{\text{SITR rate x total amount invested}}$$

Law: TCGA 1992, s. 255C

23.3 Deferral relief

23.3.1 Introduction

CGT deferral relief (sometimes referred to as "holdover relief") allows an investor to match his investment to any capital gains made within a specific time window, and defer paying the CGT on those gains until such time as the SITR investments are disposed of, or relief is otherwise withdrawn.

In order to qualify for deferral relief, the consideration payable for the SITR investment has to be eligible for income tax relief. Relief does not have to be claimed, but the tighter wording of the legislation compared to the EIS deferral relief leads to two key differences from that relief:

- investors who would be treated as connected (under the EIS provisions) cannot claim relief as they would not be eligible for income tax relief; and
- the maximum amount of gains that can be deferred in any tax year is restricted to £1 million because investment in excess of that amount would not be eligible for income tax relief.

Law: TCGA 1992, Sch. 8B

23.3.2 Further conditions

In addition to the requirement for the consideration to be eligible for income tax relief, there are five further conditions that must be met for deferral relief to be applicable. These are referred to in the legislation as conditions A to E.

Condition A is that the gain the investor is looking to defer is one which accrues on:

- the disposal of an asset;
- a qualifying business disposal; or

- a chargeable event related to SITR investments (i.e. a revived gain).

Condition B is that that gain accrues between 6 April 2014 and 5 April 2019 (the cut-off for this period may be extended in a later Finance Bill).

Condition C is that the investor is resident in the UK at the time when the gain to be deferred accrues, and when the social holding is acquired.

Condition D is that the social holding is acquired by the investor on the investor's own behalf.

Condition E is that the social holding is acquired within the time period beginning 12 months before the gain accrual time, and ending three years afterwards.

Law: TCGA 1992, Sch. 8B, para. 1

23.3.3 Reviving gains

Once deferral relief has been made following a qualifying investment in assets, the gain accruing is deferred until a chargeable event occurs. The gain is simply suspended until that time.

A chargeable event occurs if, following the qualifying investment:

- the investor disposes of the assets otherwise than to a spouse or civil partner;
- a spouse or civil partner who has received the assets on a no gain no loss basis disposes of the assets;
- the asset is cancelled, extinguished, redeemed, or repaid; or
- any of the ongoing conditions that must be met in respect of the investor being a qualifying investor, or the social enterprise being a qualifying social enterprise, ceases to be met.

Where there is a mixed holding, i.e. investments which attract income tax relief only, deferral relief only, or both, the share identification rules discussed in **22.2.4** must be used to identify holdings correctly, and thereby to determine which (if any) gains are to be revived upon a chargeable event.

Table of legislation

Index of cases

General index

Social Investment Tax Relief

Printed and bound in Great Britain by
Marston Book Services Limited, Oxfordshire